St. Joseph: Shadow of the Father

*In order to arrive at that which you do not know,
You must go by a way that you do not know.*

St. John of the Cross

S A I N T
JOSEPH
Shadow of the Father

Andrew Doze

Translated by
Florestine Audett, RJM

ALBA · HOUSE   N E W · Y O R K

SOCIETY OF ST. PAUL, 2187 VICTORY BLVD., STATEN ISLAND, NY 10314

ST PAULS

Library of Congress Cataloging-in-Publication Data

Doze, Andrew.
   [Joseph. English]
    Saint Joseph: shadow of the Father / Andrew Doze: [translated
by Florestine Audett].
      p.   cm.
   Translation of: Joseph.
   ISBN 0-8189-0644-8
   1. Joseph, Saint.   I. Title.
   BT690.D69   1992
   232.9'32 — dc20   92-15022
                                    CIP

Produced and designed in the United States of America by the
Fathers and Brothers of the Society of St. Paul,
2187 Victory Boulevard, Staten Island, New York 10314,
as part of their communications apostolate.

Printing Information:

Current Printing - first digit   3 4 5 6 7 8 9 10 11 12

Year of Current Printing - first year shown

1999 2000 2001 2002 2003 2004 2005 2006 2007 2008 2009

To all those, men and women,
whose trusting friendship
has been this manger
where the Mother of God
was able to lay down her Child
in Joseph's shadow.

Abbreviations

OLD TESTAMENT

Genesis	Gn	Proverbs	Pr
Exodus	Ex	Ecclesiastes	Ec
Leviticus	Lv	Song of Songs	Sg
Numbers	Nb	Wisdom	Ws
Deuteronomy	Dt	Sirach	Si
Joshua	Jos	Isaiah	Is
Judges	Jg	Jeremiah	Jr
Ruth	Rt	Lamentations	Lm
1 Samuel	1 S	Baruch	Ba
2 Samuel	2 S	Ezekiel	Ezk
1 Kings	1 K	Daniel	Dn
2 Kings	2 K	Hosea	Ho
1 Chronicles	1 Ch	Joel	Jl
2 Chronicles	2 Ch	Amos	Am
Ezra	Ezr	Obadiah	Ob
Nehemiah	Ne	Jonah	Jon
Tobit	Tb	Micah	Mi
Judith	Jdt	Nahum	Na
Esther	Est	Habakkuk	Hab
1 Maccabees	1 M	Zephaniah	Zp
2 Maccabees	2 M	Haggai	Hg
Job	Jb	Malachi	Ml
Psalms	Ps	Zechariah	Zc

NEW TESTAMENT

Matthew	Mt	1 Timothy	1 Tm
Mark	Mk	2 Timothy	2 Tm
Luke	Lk	Titus	Tt
John	Jn	Philemon	Phm
Acts	Ac	Hebrews	Heb
Romans	Rm	James	Jm
1 Corinthians	1 Cor	1 Peter	1 P
2 Corinthians	2 Cor	2 Peter	2 P
Galatians	Gal	1 John	1 Jn
Ephesians	Ep	2 John	2 Jn
Philippians	Ph	3 John	3 Jn
Colossians	Col	Jude	Jude
1 Thessalonians	1 Th	Revelation	Rv
2 Thessalonians	2 Th		

Foreword

AT the beginning of the Second Vatican Council, a Yugoslav bishop, prompted by the Spirit of the Lord, stood up and remarked that Joseph was too neglected in the teaching of the Church. The response? A general burst of laughter! So that was it: bishops had been summoned from all the corners of the world to listen to this kind of talk! Like Sarah's laughter behind Abraham's tent, this peal of laughter entered into history . . . perhaps it even rose up to the throne of the Most High: the answer was not slow in coming. On the following day, Tuesday, November 13, 1962, Cardinal Cicognani, speaking for the Pope, announced that the Holy Father had decided to introduce St. Joseph into the canon of the Roman Mass.

This was a bold move. To dare touch the venerable canon that went as far back as Pope Pius V at the end of the sixteenth century! But John XXIII was thereby giving expression to his innermost thought: he had placed the Council in the hands of his dear St. Joseph on March 19, 1961, during a beautiful speech in which he had reviewed the acts of his predecessors since Pius IX. He had wanted the altar dedicated to St. Joseph in St. Peter's basilica to be particularly embellished and become a center of attraction for Christians.[1]

But, above all, the Pope was fulfilling the wish of a young Dominican, Father Jean-Joseph Lataste, who had died as a saintly man at the age of thirty-seven in 1869 and offered his life so that Joseph might be given his rightful place in the Church and, especially, that his name might be listed in the canon of the Mass.

Besides, this Father Lataste himself had had a personal relationship with St. Joseph. He had taken his name in memory of St. John-Joseph of the Cross, a Neapolitan Franciscan, who constantly repeated: ''God is a kind Father who loves and helps his children.'' Father Lataste himself was to exercise this loving fatherhood toward the women prisoners of the *Maison Centrale* of Cadillac in Gironde during a memorable retreat he preached in September 1864. The outcome of this retreat was the establishment of the *Maison de Béthanie;*[2] its special work was to help women prisoners, who wanted to change their lives, by making a break with their miserable world. Through his experience, Father Lataste had entered into the mystery of St. Joseph.

Indeed, experience is the only way one can penetrate into this mystery. Joseph remains silent and the Bible says so little about him. Some saints, such as St. Teresa of Avila, had this experience. She was convinced that Joseph played a most important role and, indeed, she could see this in her own life. One of her contemporaries, the theologian Francisco de Suarez, had understood that St. Joseph had his place in the incarnation as the Virgin Mary had hers, that his place was unique among the other saints and his role much greater than was generally believed.

As soon as we focus our own mind on the absolutely exceptional responsibilities of this humble man of the tribe of David, on the occasion of the incarnation of the Son of God, we can no longer perceive things as we did before. We sense a mystery and, with the least little help from the Lord in the form of some encounter, some interesting text, some striking experience, our conviction grows stronger. We do not understand but we undergo a kind of experience, and we are determined to walk in the footsteps of Jesus who discovered human fatherhood through this man. Jesus knew, better than anyone, that ''from [the Father] every family in heaven and on earth takes its name'' (Ep 3:15).

When we are introduced to the mystery of Joseph we also quickly understand an essential point. We realize that Mary has a most important role to play in the discovery of Joseph. She sets Jesus himself directly on the new road when she tells him: "Your father and I have been searching for you" (Lk 2:48).

Indeed, one must make a journey in the very footsteps of Jesus: the effect of these words is that Jesus accepts to make a disconcerting descent. This descent strikes me very much personally and I would like others to share the remarkable impression it makes on me. I am deeply convinced that Mary is saying to each one of us these few words we have often read or heard without attention: "Your father and I have been searching for you. . . ." What do they mean? Jesus himself does not appear to have accepted them straightaway! As a result of these words, his whole person will, as it were, keel over, from a high point of splendor to an apparently lowly, pitiable one where his Father is waiting for him, where his Father wants him to be for so many years. If Mary is speaking to me also in these same terms, as I cannot help but believe, what does she wish to tell me? What must I do?

It is to answer these questions that I have launched myself into the adventure of which this book is the corresponding evidence.

This book is divided into seven chapters organized around the fourth one, out of respect for a symbolic process so often present in the Bible. To begin with, the Creation narrative is divided into seven days of which the fourth day is, as it were, the key day. It was on this day that God created the great lights of heaven, the sun, the moon, and the stars to deck the heavens. They are so called because the names of these dominating luminaries recall divinities of the idolatrous peoples surrounding the Hebrews. The sun gives light to the earth and makes human life possible; as for the moon which presides over night, it will make the computation of time possible. These heavenly bodies reflected the light born on the first day and allow us to calculate when the day of the Sabbath will be, this great day when man is invited to be again with his Creator, the last day of creation. Thus, as God has wished, Wednesday refers both to Sunday and to Saturday; it is the middle day.

Similarly, the fourth phase of our journey, the descent of Jesus from Jerusalem to Nazareth, must shed a new light on the first three phases which are a meditation on the history of Christian thought, and on the last three, which attempt to outline a mode of life and thought, in line with the rather astonishing discoveries we will be led to make.

How then can we know Joseph? Certainly not by means of rational operations of the kind theologians[3] use as a rule. Only a humble, simple union with Christ can gradually bring about some elements of an answer. It is in Jesus alone, under Mary's guidance, that one may attempt to speak about Joseph.

What helped me in this research is first my experience in life and, in a very special way, the ministry of confession at the shrine of Lourdes. Then, two women, St. Teresa of Avila and St. Bernadette, not to speak of the Virgin Mary who is constantly present.

In a very particular way, St. Bernadette gave me a glimpse of all I am trying to say here, that I have never heard nor read before. She is much more than the humble messenger of the Queen of Heaven. Indeed, she would have been happy just to report the words she had heard and set humankind on the road to conversion but her whole life points to a profound journey yet to be discovered. She is, as has been rightly said, "the first and the true sign of Lourdes,"[4] expressed through her entire life, first in Lourdes and then in Nevers.

My attempt goes back to profound aspirations like those of Francis Jammes, the poet, who in the '20s invoked St. Joseph in these words: "You, the man who has been scoffed at, whose name alone is a source of embarrassment on the lips of the lukewarm Christian and a blasphemy on those of the impious . . . accept my homage. Your humility moves me as the wind moves the deep waters. But speak to me in ways other than this mysterious silence! Reveal yourself to me, in this work, in ways other than in paper and plaster images. You must truly live in my heart, in my writings."[5]

Only one thing matters: to give, under Mary's inspiration, full
significance to the invitation made by Philip to Nathanael at the
beginning of John's Gospel: "We have found him about whom
Moses in the law and also the prophets wrote, Jesus of Nazareth,
the son of Joseph. — Can anything good come out of Nazareth? —
Come and see!" (Jn 1:45-46).

1 *Documentation Catholique*, 1961, p. 417.
2 Bresson will draw the plot of his film *Les anges du péché* from the life led in one of the
houses of Bethany and the human problems experienced there.
3 As, for example, Father Lallement (died 1977) who admits having sought to penetrate
the mystery of the fatherhood of Joseph "for twenty or thirty years . . . amid all sorts of
anxieties" (*La paternité de Joseph*, Téqui, 1986).
4 Fr. Bordes, *Journal de la Grotte*, 4 March 1973, p. 2.
5 M. d'Hartoy, *Le grand péché des catholiques*, Aubanel, 1948, p. 56.

Preface

CLEMENT of Alexandria, while explaining his work, the *Stromateis* (which means "the Tapestries"), defined his objective as follows:

"Plants displaying their variety of fruit in meadows are not separated from each other according to species. Similarly, some writers have recorded the assorted results of their learned gleanings in anthologies entitled *Meadows, Wreaths, Honeycombs, Interweaves. . . .* We have embroidered the design of these Tapestries in the style of a meadow" (*Stromateis* VI, 1, 2, 1).

One will find that this book, displaying little of the academic and reflecting an Eastern rather than a Western influence, suggests something of the "Tapestries." Flowers of diverse species make up its bouquet: biblical meditations, echoes of pastoral experience, reflections of personal prayer, the significant presence of men and women of the Church, of thinkers, of saints are all gathered together in an ornamental filigree around St. Joseph's personality.

Perhaps it would be more exact to say, as the author repeats, that everything is orchestrated around God the Father. Indeed, Jesus discovered human fatherhood through Joseph. The Gospel word "*Abba*," Father, whispered by this most loving Son even in the throes of his final agony, is the witness and echo of his filial relationship with the First Person of the Blessed Trinity.

Reflecting, in turn, rabbinical, Alexandrian, and Carmelite influences, including that of Lourdes, the author teaches us to live in the company of Joseph "who creates, protects and directs Mary's home" and "who is for Jesus the face of the eternal Father." He wants to give us a Christian way of life through Joseph, "a certain way of perceiving things, of walking, of breathing, a way that involves the feet and the hands."

For him, to become a son of Joseph is to imitate what the Father in heaven does (Jn 5:19). It is a very simple way of managing one's life by putting humble observances into practice. It means to filter threatening influences through silence and darkness and to decant one's human experience. It means to make the world of today, which suffers so much from "a fatherhood shirking its obligations," benefit from the experience of Joseph, the foster father "who brings the fatherhood from heaven down to this earth."

People will be grateful to the Chaplain of Lourdes for having elaborated a spiritual doctrine from the words of Bernadette: "Don't you know that now Joseph is my father?" This was in August 1872, seven years before her death. Already, huge crowds of pilgrims were on the move, eager to follow the same itinerary as Mary and Joseph: to find the Son and a childlike soul in the house of the Father.

"I bow my knees before the Father, from whom every family in heaven and on earth takes its name . . . so that you may be filled with all the fullness of God" (Ep 3:14ff).

PIERRE MOLÉRES
Bishop of Bayonne, Lescar and Oloron

Contents

St. Joseph: Shadow of the Father

CHAPTER I

A Progressive Revelation

"BLESSED be the God and Father of our Lord Jesus Christ, who has blessed us in Christ with every spiritual blessing" (Ep 1:3). St. Paul thus begins his Letter to the Ephesians which contains an admirable hymn to Christ. All things come from the Father in Christ. All things are restored in Christ: the gigantic convulsions of creation, the choice of the Jewish nation, the incarnation of the Son, his life, his death, his resurrection, his ascension, the existence and the life of the Church, all things converge on Christ and Christ is totally turned toward the Father. "When all things are subjected to him, then the Son himself will also be subjected to the one who put all things in subjection under him, so that God may be all in all" (1 Cor 15:28).

"Like Christ who during his life on earth was aware that he came from the Father and was going back to the Father (cf. Jn 13:1), the Church must become more deeply aware that she comes from the Father and that she is moving toward him."[1]

The time spent in the desert in the life of the Chosen People is like a shortened version of this vast history which continues to unfold itself: "You saw how the Lord your God carried you, just as one carries a child, all the way that you travelled until you reached this place" (Dt 1:31). This Father is a loving father "like those who lift infants to their cheeks" (Ho 11:4) but, at the same time, he is as demanding as a true father should be, training his son by putting him to the test and supporting him (cf Dt 8:5). The law given to the people in the midst of this life in the desert has no other function, as St. Paul says, but to be this pedagogue agreeing to wait for the moment of blessing when humanity, in the Holy Spirit, will finally be able to cry out: Abba! Father! The Spirit of the Son will inspire them at last (cf Gal 3:24; 4:6).

All of history is therefore but a slow journey, often tragic and inconsistent, for it is free, moving toward this discovery that changes everything: we too, poor humans, can call God our Father! It is in Christ that we can be introduced to these wonders by the Holy Spirit he gives us. "Being therefore exalted at the right hand of God, and having received from the Father the promise of the Holy Spirit, he has poured out this" (Ac 2:33).

The coming of Jesus and the slow process of shaping his personality are linked with Mary and Joseph, this couple that we must learn no longer to separate, since God has united it.

The revelation of the person and role of St. Joseph is correlated in a special and peculiar way, which goes unnoticed, with the revelation of the eternal Father. One does not occur without the other. We shall see this in Jesus' own experience.

Beyond a doubt, this revelation is made gradually according to the will of the eternal Father from whom all things come, as St. James ponders: "Do not be deceived, my beloved. Every generous act of giving, with every perfect gift, is from above, coming down from the Father of lights, with whom there is no variation or shadow due to change" (Jm 1:16-17). The consideration of the main stages of this revelation is very instructive.

1. A LONG NIGHT

Initial Obscurity

Our study begins in the night. Whereas St. Mark's gospel gives many details on the life of Jesus, the name of Joseph does not appear. One could think that the other evangelists do not give him any importance either: but this is not the case. The few passages about Joseph in Luke and Matthew are, on the contrary, of utmost importance, but this importance is concealed. As for St. John, he devotes a significant verse to the discovery of the Messiah in chapter 1 of his gospel: "We have found him," says Philip triumphantly, speaking of the One foretold by Moses and the prophets, "[he is] Jesus, son of Joseph, from Nazareth" (Jn 1:45). Obviously, he was well hidden!

Everything happens as if the eternal Father had wanted this man to play his role fully but not visibly. He is the son of David by whom Jesus will legitimately bear his illustrious title designating him as the Messiah. He is the husband of the Blessed Virgin and nothing is more striking than this evident fact which generally goes unnoticed. The annunciation is related by St. Luke in such a way that his name appears before that of Mary. Mary is a young girl described only in terms of her betrothal to Joseph, this young man of the tribe of David, "and the virgin's name was Mary." This name Joseph is that of a famous patriarch who, in the past, saved the people of God in Egypt and the name of Mary, forever blessed, sounds only as an echo of the first. But Joseph immediately withdraws from the scene.

Nevertheless, one feels his presence everywhere in the Infancy Narratives of the gospels. An active, vigilant, necessary presence: through the ministry of the angel of the Lord, he is put in charge of specific tasks, whether it is to go to Bethlehem, his native city where the Child is to be born, or to organize this birth, or to give this child the name of Jesus, a whole program in itself, since it means Savior.

When the powers of death threaten the Child, he alone is warned, but with what discretion! In the night, in a dream, like the ones we could all have. As soon as Mary is mentioned, and Joseph perhaps still more so, everything is both divine and simple.

After the scene of paramount importance in the temple, in

chapter 2 of St. Luke, when Jesus goes down with his parents, Joseph disappears at the same time as Jesus and Mary or, rather, Jesus and Mary disappear thanks to him. He keeps in the background and conceals at the same time. He is hidden and he hides. His name is the present participle of the Hebrew verb meaning "to increase" and "to cut off." The two meanings of the word fully interplay: Jesus will "increase" in Joseph's safekeeping, he will increase astonishingly; "Jesus increased in wisdom, and in years, and in divine and human favor" (Lk 2:52). Joseph has the authority to do that (we know that the root of the word "authority" is precisely that, augere, meaning "to increase," "to cause to grow"). But truly, what first strikes us about Joseph is a certain way of "cutting back," of taking away. He takes away the incarnation from our view. Bossuet expressed this magnificently: "The apostles are lights to show Jesus Christ to the world; Joseph is a veil to cover him and, behind this veil, are hidden Mary's virginity and the greatness of the Savior of souls."[2]

To hide, to cover, to take away, by removing this child entrusted to him by the Father from a hostile or immature world: that is the first strong impression the gospel makes on us when we are searching for Joseph there. But let us not forget the essential. Surprised by the events, Joseph was ready to separate, and how painfully so, from this young fiancée, unique of her kind, whom he undoubtedly had known for a long time and who must have inspired in him the kind of love we can imagine. How could he, the poor man, be involved in circumstances which were totally beyond him, where he felt the finger of God? Without that, since he was "a righteous man," as Scripture tells us, his duty was to denounce Mary.

This tragedy and the agonizing pain accompanying it, no doubt, provide the angel with the opportunity to make an astonishing revelation: "Joseph, son of David, do not be afraid to take Mary as your wife, for the child conceived in her is from the Holy Spirit" (Mt 1:20). All the Church will be able to do is to understand progressively the meaning of this verse which contains everything: the Holy Spirit begets the body of Christ in Mary, but Mary must dwell with Joseph. The meaning of this expression is what must be better understood, with the help of the Lord.

The fact that Joseph was preparing to say "no" to a mystery which was beyond him and of which he felt himself unworthy, is significant. God invites him to pronounce, with his whole being, a silent "yes" which echoes throughout eternity, a "yes" whose impact is considerable like everything that directly touches the incarnation.

Then Joseph discreetly withdraws from the context of the gospel when his son reaches the age of thirty. This is the age when the Joseph of ancient times takes his leave from the Pharaoh to begin his brilliant career as prime minister (cf Gn 41:46). It is the age when David, the beloved forefather, becomes king (cf 2 S 5:4), the age of heavy responsibilities. The reason for this silent disappearance, later imitated by Mary, is simple: henceforth, Jesus will speak of the Father as the center of his whole mission. There must not be the slightest ambiguity. Joseph must in no way perturb this mission. Not only does he not say a single word in the whole gospel (he expresses himself in other ways), but he must no longer be spoken of as the "father of Jesus" in the way Mary had done openly in the temple in Jerusalem, in the the way that the people of Galilee (the people from up North!) who had known him as a young boy were still doing when he began to preach. When they heard his rather intolerable remarks on the Bread of Life, "the Jews began to complain about him because he said, 'I am the bread that came down from heaven.' They were saying, 'Is not this Jesus, the son of Joseph, whose father and mother we know? How can he now say, I have come down from heaven?' " (Jn 6:41-42).

Joseph had to disappear, at least seemingly, to clear the way for the revelation par excellence, the revelation of the eternal Father. In fact, we shall see, he is present in a particular way, but let us not anticipate.

Divine Pedagogy

"I pray that the God of our Lord Jesus Christ, the Father of glory, may give you a spirit of wisdom and revelation as you come to know him. . . . And he has put all things under his feet and has made him the head over all things for the church" (Ep 1:17, 22). All reality culminates in Chirst and "no one knows . . . who the Father is except the Son and anyone to whom the Son chooses to reveal him" (Lk 10:22).

In the Son, we have all things, but this was revealed gradually. St. Gregory of Nazianzus explains why: men could not bear too much light at one time, they would have confused everything. That is why long periods of time were necessary.

One can discern three ages of the world and of grace: the age of the Father before the Church, the age of the Son on whom everything converges, the age of the Holy Spirit pouring the grace of Christ on the world. "They correspond to the three manifestations of the three divine persons professed in the Creed, in which creation is linked with the Father, the redeeming incarnation with the Son, the birth and the catholicity of the Church with the Spirit. The ultimate parousia will not inaugurate a fourth age of the world and of grace: it will manifest the transfiguring virtue and the splendor of the grace deposited in the world on the day of Pentecost. Christ appears at the center of the history of time, at the end of the second age of the world and before the third, between the annunciation and the ascension. He is above the Church and the times of the Church."[3]

It all began with the revelation of the Father. Humanity had to understand not only that God exists but that there is only one God, a fact which is much more difficult to accept. We willingly believe in the existence of forces superior to ourselves, which must be cajoled, won to our side: this is the most fundamental principle underlying religious efforts, the most universal in life. The deep significance of the vocation of Abraham and of the people coming from him is profoundly original with respect to this religious instinct of humanity. Men will no longer try to subdue all these gods of which they have a confused notion in order to win their favor and to enlist their services. On the contrary, they will learn to listen to the one true God who takes the initiative of the word. The Jewish people, as it were, is seized by God. It is surrounded by numerous idolatrous peoples who want to fit their gods into their plans and schemes. What a constant temptation to imitate them! It would be so much easier, so much more profitable, at least so it seems!

Gradually, after the horrendous ordeals it undergoes, the relentless warnings from the prophets, the training of the men of God, the Chosen People accepts what God says of himself: "I am the first and I am the last; besides me there is no god. Who is like me? Let them proclaim it, let them declare and set it forth before me" (Is 44:6-7).

What a profound topic of meditation it is just to consider this truth: on the one hand, divine revelation ties in with the profound aspirations of humanity; on the other, humanity, more often than not, seems to open up to this revelation only by resisting it with all its might!

Then came the period of the Son. The first centuries of the Church are characterized by the terrible struggles against the heresy spread by Arius.

Arius perceived Christ as a superior creature but he did not believe that Christ was God, therefore, equal with the Father, the Second Person of the Blessed Trinity, a mystery that was being gradually discovered. He was an intelligent man, even brilliant; he spoke rationally, in the human way, in the religiously human way of men. The Father is above, like the emperor on whose will everything hangs at the political level; then comes the Son, a superior creature but lesser than the Father, as he says so of himself (cf Jn 14:28),[4] then come the angels, duly categorized into hierarchies; then men who are no less so. A well-ordered world.

St. Paul affirms that the wisdom of God is folly in the eyes of men, and that men relying solely on the light of their reason "do not receive the gifts of God's Spirit" (1 Cor 2:14). This is folly, for we cannot open up to this except by going against the current of what we usually think and what we would think, were we left solely to our reasoning. The text of the Nicene Creed (381) affirms this incredible truth which neither the Jews nor the Muslims accept: Jesus, this man born of Mary, is God. He is equal with the Father. No truth is more baffling than that one, more shocking to human reason. No truth is more astonishing, more fruitful, more dynamic when it is accepted in faith.

And the Holy Spirit? The fact that our Creed does not directly affirm the divinity of the Spirit is striking. He is presented as God because we worship him in union with the Father and the Son. We worship him; therefore, he is God. St. Athanasius states, in the same frame of mind, that he is God since he deifies us. Nothing shows better the extent to which divine truth does not emerge from brilliant deductions as science does, but imposes itself in the course of an obscure encounter between God and man, comes as the result of an indescribable experience, a loving attraction. It is in the night of faith that this Holy Spirit operates and reveals "the whole truth" to us, as Jesus promised, and "pours love into our hearts" (cf Rm 5:5). This is the way by which he deifies us.

As soon as the mystery of God begins to appear more clearly, people may show interest in the Virgin Mary. Actually, the degree to which her mystery was linked to that of Jesus was felt from the start. The impassioned debates on the human and divine nature of Christ in the fifth century will provide the occasion for the Council of Ephesus (431) to proclaim that Mary is "the Mother of God" much to the joy of the Christian people. People often sense the truth from within. But it took many centuries to admit at last that she was totally shielded from sin, even from original sin. The Eastern Church began to celebrate this privilege in about the eighth century but the Western World, much given to rational debates, took longer to accept this belief. After ten centuries of quarreling and confrontation, Pope Pius IX ran the risk of proclaiming the dogma of the Immaculate Conception on December 8, 1854. Actually, he was supported by the entire Church and strongly impelled to do so by the apparitions of the Rue du Bac in 1830.

And Joseph

Providence chose to keep him in a most complete obscurity during the first centuries of Christianity. Better yet: it, as it were, blurred traces of him. In our modern jargon, we would say that the operation was one of "misinformation." To misinform is to spread false rumors the better to lead people astray. Thus, James' Protoevangelium (a venerated text written for edification purposes but in a style in contrast with that of the Gospel, so sparing of words, so respectful of sources) invents details about Mary and Joseph. Joseph is presented as an old man who has already been married and has had children with a former wife. That simplified everything: Mary's virginity had a good custodian. At the same time, one could explain the presence of "the brothers of Jesus," a source of such embarrassment for those who are not familiar with the Semitic way of so designating members of a clan.

These distorted images were to circulate throughout the entire Middle Ages and they continue more or less to command attention in the Eastern Church, which is much more sensitive to the impact of ancient texts than we Westerners. Such is the origin of the imagery which presents this young Jew in the guise of a pensive old man, retreated in the corner of pictures, fulfilling a function which is obviously beyond him, his role being reduced to enhancing the presence of his radiant wife.[5]

Fortunately, already during the first centuries, some thinking was being called for: Joseph and Mary were truly married and here, less than elsewhere, what God had united could not be separated. It is the appearance of the man and the woman, this couple whom the Creator demands to be but one sole reality, that the inspired author considers to be the image and the likeness of God. At the same time, that is the condition of all human life on earth and the true introduction into the knowledge of the divine mysteries: for this reason, Jesus, to the strong indignation of the apostles, recalls in Matthew 19 that the marriage of man and woman, faithful, indissoluble, is the key to the beginnings he has just restored. The history of ancient societies and of the Middle Ages, such as it is now reconstructed, shows the extent to which this exacting demand imposed by Christ appeared difficult. The Council of Trent and men like St. Francis de Sales initiated a profound reflection, but it is only in the twentieth century that the reality of marriage as a mystery and as a way to holiness stands out in a new light.[6]

This historical evolution prevents the couple, Joseph and Mary, from having the importance it will eventually have when God is willing — but the reality of such a union commands attention. St. Augustine, an observer so exacting in the matter of sin, casts the idea aside when it applies to the Mother of God and he has to admit that Joseph's virginity is, as it were, a condition for that of his wife. St. Ambrose and St. John Chrysostom will not separate Joseph from Mary when they meditate on the absolutely exceptional holiness of this woman God chose to be the New Eve.

Can we really speak of the holiness of the one without necessarily thinking of the holiness of the other, her inseparable companion who was but one with her? And so, already at the dawn of Christianity, the principles that Pope Leo XIII developed in *Quamquam pluries* (1889) are laid down: Joseph and Mary are married and Joseph's holiness is mysteriously akin to that of Mary.[7] "And behold at the threshold of the New Testament, as at the entrance to the Old, a married couple stands. But whereas Adam and Eve were the source of evil unleashed on the world, Joseph and Mary are the summit whence holiness spreads all over the earth."[8]

The Middle Ages

In the first half of the twelfth century, we meet the great St. Bernard, this devoted lover of Mary. While meditating on the annunciation, his favorite subject, in the presence of his monks, he catches sight of Joseph and, through his own experience, he senses the reason why Joseph wanted to dismiss his pregnant wife: "Joseph . . . judging that he too (like the centurion before Jesus) was an unworthy sinner, was saying to himself: 'She is so perfect and so great that I do not deserve to share her intimacy any longer; her astonishing dignity is beyond me, it frightens me.' He could see with awesome fear that she was bearing the very clear sign of a divine presence."

St. Bernard understands that this man is God's steward who, by the very fact, eminently transcends the ancient Joseph who was but the intendant of Pharaoh, a distant image of the Master of the Holy Family. Joseph was able to see with his own eyes, to hold in his arms and to shower with kisses the one whom "so many kings and prophets had hoped to see and did not see."

What St. Bernard does not understand so well is precisely the exact significance of Joseph and Mary's marriage and, consequently, of Joseph's fatherhood with respect to Jesus which stems from this marriage (Joseph becomes Jesus' father because he is Mary's husband). "He (Joseph) was neither the husband of the mother nor the father of the son, and yet an unquestionable and necessary plan forced him to bear for a while this double title of husband and father and to be considered as such."[9]

These reticences are interesting and show, better than anything else, how the mystery of Joseph remains hidden "by an unquestionable and necessary plan," again according to St. Bernard's own terms.

A few years later, St. Francis of Assisi, whose passionate soul wanted to follow Jesus in every one of his footsteps, instinctively rediscovers Joseph's role when he wants to relive the radiant poverty of the Nativity during the Night at Greccio on Christmas 1223 toward the end of his life. The poor like him are at home in Joseph's world. His young disciple, the Portuguese Anthony of Padua, the most popular of all the Latin saints, will be represented holding the Child Jesus in his arms as if he were, in fact, without anyone planning this, the first living icon of the young Joseph. No saint will be as quickly recognized as such: because of his numerous miracles, Anthony was declared a saint the year following his death.

We have there, as it were, a popular and profound experience of the mystery of the Holy Family which will appear again in St. Bonaventure's thought (for whom, however, St. Joseph still remains "a holy old man"!) and, especially so in acts of devotion. The first liturgical offices in honor of our saint will appear among the Franciscans. A Franciscan pope, Sixtus IV, is the one who introduced St. Joseph into the breviary and set his first liturgical feast in the Church by the Act of November 19, 1480. The first chapel erected in his honor is undoubtedly the one built by the Franciscans in Toulouse in 1222. Along the same line, the first great promoters of his cause, if we can speak in this way, are Franciscans such as Bernardino of Siena in Italy and Cardinal Cisneros in Spain at the time St. Teresa was born.[10]

Beyond any question, through all sorts of witnesses, by all sorts of signs, a new interest manifests itself for this secretive man, so profoundly hidden, whom the Father has chosen for great things. A privileged witness is undoubtedly Ubertino of Casale, an Italian of the end of the thirteenth century who was a Benedictine at one time. Exiled in 1305 on Mount Alvernia, where eighty years earlier St. Francis had received the stigmata, he meditated on the mysteries of Jesus and hence he met Joseph. In his work, *Arbor vitae crucifixae*, he expresses what should become the basic intuition of Christian thought: Mary is perfectly sanctified by Jesus, and Joseph is perfectly sanctified through the intermediacy of Mary.

"In every marriage, the union of hearts is achieved to such a

point that the husband and wife are called one and the same person
[*sic*, it would be preferable to say, along with the Bible, one same
flesh, one same reality in two persons]. Hence, Joseph cannot help
but be like the Blessed Virgin, his wife. How then could a penetrating mind think that the Holy Spirit would have joined to the soul of
a virgin like Mary another soul, in so close a union, unless the
practice of virtue had made Joseph's soul very similar to hers? I
hold it for certain that St. Joseph was therefore the most purely
virgin man, the most profoundly humble, the most elevated in
contemplation.''[11]

Then comes a startling meditation, which St. Francis de Sales
will take up again in precisely the same terms, as if he had copied it,
on Jesus in the arms of Joseph, experiencing through him the love
of the Father:

"Oh! What sweet kisses he received from him! Oh! How
pleasant it was to hear him as a tiny child call him by the sweet
name of father, and with what bliss he felt his gentle embraces.
This was so because an unconditional and transforming love disposed him toward Jesus as toward a most gentle son given to him by
the Holy Spirit through the Blessed Virgin, his wife."

Indeed, for Ubertino of Casale, Joseph is the apex, "the happy
conclusion to the Ancient Law."

In a covert manner, new discoveries are being prepared for the
fifteenth and especially for the sixteenth century.

2. THE DAY IS DAWNING

The Great Commotion

Under the threefold influence of an outstanding personality, of
popular devotion and of certain events, behold, at the beginning of
the fifteenth century, the name of Joseph is emerging from the
shadows like spring breaking forth with new life. It is spectacular!

First, this is the era of popular preaching in the city of Bernardino of Siena. During a period of twenty-five years, this Franciscan friar traveled all over Italy preaching with great skill. He had a prodigious success. His love for the Lord and the Name of Jesus led him to understand the importance of the Blessed Virgin and of St. Joseph on whom he reflected most profoundly in the very line followed by Ubertino of Casale. He died in 1444 (and was canonized in 1450, so firmly was his reputation of holiness established). He had no doubts, in particular, that Joseph is in heaven, body and soul, for his role in the incarnation was so great that he necessarily had to grace the eternal registers, in heaven as on earth.

Another Italian, this time a Dominican, Isidore Isolani (died 1528) deserved to be called "the prophet of Joseph" in that northern part of Italy where he exercised his apostolate. He dedicated his masterpiece, *Somma dei doni di San Giuseppe* (1522) (A summa of the gifts of St. Joseph), to Pope Adrian VI, a work which made this author, along with his near contemporary the French Jean Gerson, the great specialist of what will later be called "Josephology." In a grandiose vision, worthy of the prophets of Israel, he foresaw the day when the Church, "in the light the angels would give" (a precious note!), would discover at least the treasures hidden by God in Joseph and "the great joy that the certain knowledge of the holiness of the divine Joseph would bring to the militant Church of the future."[12]

One of the most astonishing witnesses of this period is Jean Gerson, a person of note, the chancellor of the University of Paris, a position which earned him the distinction of being sent to the Council of Constance to represent the king of France. There, he played an important role in times that were hard. Christendom was being torn by three popes, one in Rome, one in Avignon, and a particularly intriguing third one in Pisa. The Council was to obtain their abdication and bring about a complete straightening out of the situation. In these conditions, Jean Gerson delivered a memorable address on September 8, 1416 on the nativity of Mary. This text was an excuse used basically to speak about Joseph for whom he had a great love, a deep veneration. He had understood the import-ance of the marriage of Joseph and Mary and would have liked the liturgy in the kingdom of France to honor him with a special feast. He had begged the Duke of Berry to intercede with the competent authorities: the liturgical text was ready. His speech at the Council exalted the holiness of Joseph as being concomitant with that of Mary. To praise the greatness of the one was to exalt the other.

For him, as for the other authors of these times, Joseph was a young man, active, of perfect purity, eminently holy, certainly sanctified in his mother's womb as St. John the Baptist would be. The author was convinced that he is spiritually present in heaven; "as for his body," he added, "I do not know. . . ."

This man, who used his leisure time to write Latin verses on Joseph, died at the very moment Joan of Arc was beginning to draw attention upon herself: he had been consulted about her. Two centuries later, another son of St. Joseph, St. Francis de Sales, would described him as "extremely learned, judicious, devout." A kind of kindred spirit enabled them to understand each other.

Everything was ready for the coming of the "daughter of St. Joseph," the first in the history of the Church: Teresa of Avila.

Joseph Gains A Foothold

St. Teresa ushers in an experience which must be properly assessed. She was born in 1515 and joined her beloved Jesus on October 4, 1582, the feast of St. Francis of Assisi, of whom she was especially fond. "It is time we should see each other!" she said at the moment of her death.

We shall come back to the deep significance of the contribution made by St. Teresa of Avila; for the time being let us simply determine her place in our rapidly progressing journey. Concerning Jesus, the absolute center of her life, and, therefore, also concerning those united with him, Joseph and Mary, Teresa of Avila was to play the role of the manger of Bethlehem. She would provide them with a new shelter. In a new way, they would, so to speak, gain a foothold in her and in her foundations. The fire Jesus yearned for, the fire he was so eager to kindle on the earth (Lk 12:49), this fire of divine love would be set aflame in her a new way. No one would speak in better terms than she of the stages of prayer and its summit, the spiritual nuptials.

God gave her absolutely new insights on St. Joseph. She experienced a kind of vital relationship with him which cannot help but strike one by its force, its certitude, its effectiveness. It is one thing to have had a glimpse of the eminent role played by St. Joseph as did the persons we have just spoken of; it is quite another to take him as a father with the full significance conveyed by this expression.

Teresa was of Jewish ancestry. She had lost her mother when still young and had a deep affection for her father, an exceptional man. Moreover, she was intelligent, positive, of an ardent nature, obviously chosen by God to accomplish great things.

She progressively experienced a known phenomenon which psychologists call a transfer: she transferred the profound love she had felt for Don Alonso, this loving father present to her whom God had given her, to Joseph.

In a moment of fervor, a costly one for her, she left him and entered the Carmel at the age of twenty-one. Very soon, through lack of experience, through excessive austerities and, especially, through the absence of a well-balanced spiritual direction, she was seriously taken ill. The quack woman doctor who was consulted brought her to the gates of death. At twenty-three, she was thought to be dead. Wax had been applied on her eyes and the funeral was ready. Her father alone, like a madman, kept repeating: "Oh! no, my daughter does not look like a woman ready to be placed in a casket!'' Out of pity for the distraught man, the funeral was delayed. On the third day she made an imperceptible sign. She was alive. It would take her three years to recover from that terrible shock, up to the happy day when, at last, she was able "to walk on hands and knees." Joseph was the one, she affirms, who saved her.

From that moment, he held a pre-eminent place in her life: "I found that this my father and lord delivered me both from the trouble and also from other troubles concerning my honor and the loss of my soul, and that he gave me greater blessings than I could ask of him."[13] With an astonishing piece of prose springing directly from her heart she speaks of "her father" in ways no human being under the sun had ever done before.

Undoubtedly, the most amazing aspect of this is that she considers St. Joseph as her master in prayer: "If anyone cannot find a master to teach him how to pray, let him take this glorious saint as his master and he will not go astray."[14] Teresa, the master in prayer in the Church, a Doctor on the matter, had clearly understood a truth that the Church endlessly keeps on learning: Joseph was the way to the Father, mysteriously established by God, for Mary and for Jesus himself. Joseph was the master in prayer for the Queen of angels and for the Son of Man.

That is why, at the age of forty-seven, after a long journey and a real conversion to God, it is to St. Joseph that she really entrusts this new house of prayer which the Lord was urging her to found, this small Holy Family, the convent of St. Joseph of Avila, the first Carmel monastery of the Reform. The Order of the Virgin Mary became, at the same time, the Order of St. Joseph, and Mary was profoundly happy about this change.[15]

For people coming after St. Teresa of Avila and following in her footsteps, the way, acknowledged and chosen, is mapped out. St. Francis de Sales, Jean-Jacques Olier, founder of the Society of St. Sulpice and of the first seminaries, the whole seventeenth century will be able to enter into an extraordinary intimacy with the Father's Intendant. This intimacy will find its expression in pre-eminent men: they must be heard. Nothing is more profound than the writings of Monsieur Olier; nothing is greater than the two panegyrics written by Bossuet in 1656 and 1661.[16]

Canada, the destination of the first missionaries who had just left for its shores, would become the land of St. Joseph as early as March 19, 1624 and would remain so. An ancient text (1637) expresses this forcefully: "On the day of the feast, the church was filled with people and devotion, almost like Easter Sunday, everyone glorifying God for having given us the protector and the guardian angel, so to speak, of Jesus Christ his Son to be our protector. It is, in my opinion, thanks to his help and merits that the inhabitants of New France living on the shores of the mighty St. Lawrence resolved to accept all the good customs of the Old one and refuse entrance to the evil ones." Joseph giving way to whatever is suitable and turning aside whatever is not — this, in fact, is what he did in Nazareth. He acts as a filter.

3. PIUS IX OR THE DISCREET APOTHEOSIS

The Eighteenth Century

Quietly, the eighteenth century continues to meditate on the great attributes of St. Joseph. A famous Franciscan preacher, canonized by Pius IX in 1869, St. Leonard of Porto-Maurizio (died 1751), exercised his ministry in Italy and distinguished himself by the vigorous stand he took against Jansenism. St. Joseph was his great source of inspiration: he held him up to all conditions of human existence, to all classes of society. "All Christians belong to Joseph because Jesus and Mary belonged to him."

He adds: "Rejoice, devout servants of St. Joseph, for you are close to paradise; the ladder leading up to it has but three rungs, Jesus, Mary, Joseph. Here is how one climbs up or down this ladder. As you climb up, your requests are first placed in the hands of St. Joseph, St. Joseph hands them over to Mary and Mary to Jesus. As you climb down, the responses come from Jesus, Jesus delivers them to Mary and Mary hands them over to Joseph. Jesus does everything for Mary for he is her son; Mary, as his mother, obtains everything and Joseph, as a righteous man, husband and father, can do all things."[17]

Behind this playful front lies a profound wisdom. Let us keep this intuition giving Joseph the role of this "narrow gate" mentioned in the Gospel and which, as Jesus notes, is not easy to find. Joseph is the one who must take the decision to leave, while it is night, for a distant destination. He has had to accept the particular vocation of his wife and, what is yet more astonishing, the education of the Son of God. He is the man of upheavals, of commotions, of the first steps often so difficult to take, even in little things. He is the man of death to self.

The other noteworthy admirer of Joseph in this century is St. Alphonsus Liguori (died 1787), founder of the Redemptorists. He meditates on an important idea: the growth of love in the heart of Joseph, of love for Mary, of love for Jesus. Our views are too static because they are too intellectual: love within the Holy Family was, so to speak, an ongoing discovery of every instant, an adventure. When texts speak to us of "growth" (and we know that this is the very meaning of the name of Joseph, "increasing it"), what can we think of that is more worthy of growth than love?

"Among humans, the effect of living together is that we usually end up by having only a very mediocre love for each other because, as relationships are kept up, we become more and more aware of each other's shortcomings. On the contrary, as St. Joseph continued to live with Jesus, he constantly grew in admiration for his holiness. We can thereby understand what burning love he managed to have for him, having lived in this intimacy, which defies description, for no less than twenty-five years, as is generally believed.

"Noble St. Joseph, I rejoice that God found you worthy of

holding this eminent position whereby, established as the father of Jesus, you saw the one whose orders heaven and earth obey subjecting himself to your authority; since a God has wanted to obey you, allow me to be in your service, to honor you and love you as my Lord and Master.''[18]

This text raises an important question: is this a pious exaggeration like the ones "mystics" (in the pejorative sense often attached to this word) are used to make, in which case this text would become meaningless? Or, on the contrary, is this a basic statement declared by a Doctor of the Church, who has picked up the admirable legacy of the seventeenth century? In other words, St. Alphonsus would seem to understand, "to know," a truth of which the Church is still unconsciously enjoying the benefit in the way young children do: St. Joseph's role in our "entrance into the Kingdom," in our being born of the Spirit (cf Jn 3:5-6).

This question is linked to another question which is the basic direction of our meditation: if it is true that Joseph's holiness like that of Mary comes from the Blood of Christ, "the one mediator between God and humankind" (1 Tm 2:5), we may suppose that the Immaculate Virgin had, in Christ, a direct influence on the sanctification of her husband. How did Jesus himself, as man, receive from the Father from whom "comes every perfect gift" (cf Jm 1:17) the very fabric of his life at the very time when he was subjected to Mary and especially to Joseph? The answer to this question is not a theoretical one: the closer we get to Christ, the greater will be our union with him and the nearer we will come to his profound experience.

No one has meditated more admirably on these truths than the writer Ernest Hello, one hundred years after Alphonsus: "He (Joseph) was in command. The mother and the child obeyed. It seems to me that being in command must have inspired Joseph with astounding thoughts. It seems to me that the name of Jesus must have held amazing secrets for him. It seems to me that when he gave orders his humility must have grown into gigantic proportions, immeasurable against feelings we know. His humility must have matched his silence in its abysmal depths. His silence and his humility must have grown, each leaning on the other.''[19]

Indeed, if Joseph's holiness comes from Jesus, that of Jesus comes through Joseph. How can that be? The Lord will make this understood if he wishes to. Pius IX's pontificate offers the beginning of an answer to this important question.

The First Official Steps

Indeed, it was up to Pius IX to begin to promote St. Joseph officially or, more precisely, to raise slightly the veil hiding the reality, for the Church does not invent her definitions; she tries to express what God discloses to her.

Pius IX's heart was turned to Joseph: as a young priest, in 1823, in the church of St. Ignatius in Rome, he had preached a novena and a panegyric of worth in his honor, which we still have today.[20] Scarcely had he been raised to the pontifical throne when, on September 10, 1847, the pope hastened to extend a feast in honor of the patronage of St. Joseph to the whole Church, a feast which had been introduced in 1680 in Spanish and Italian Carmelite circles. In 1864, the emperor of Austria had requested in vain that this patronage should be recognized. Pius IX was to do much better: he was going to take advantage of a strong movement supported by numerous petitions to proclaim officially the patronage of St. Joseph over the universal Church on December 8, 1870 in the grandiose setting of the Vatican Council. Thus, exactly sixteen years after his wife's Immaculate Conception had been proclaimed on December 8, 1854, Joseph was receiving his first official consecration of the Church.

Nothing could have been more in agreement with the heart of the Sovereign Pontiff but he was acting not *motu proprio* but only on his own authority. A strong movement was supporting his initiative. Dating from 1815 under Pius VII, the movement wanted Joseph's name to appear in the canon of the Mass and in other official prayers of the Church. It wanted him to be named before St. John the Baptist in the litanies of the saints.

The First Fruits

The first fruits of such a fervor were not slow in coming. One is struck by the fact that all sorts of Fraternities, Confraternities, Congregations, devotions, provincial councils came into existence during the nineteenth century, all of them dedicated to St. Joseph.

These councils, in particular, testify to a true spiritual veneration, for it is not possible that the organization of these types of gatherings in the Austro-Hungarian Empire, Colombia, the United States and France could have happened by sheer chance.

Let us consider the Council of Bordeaux in 1868:[21] the participants became clearly aware that they were entering into this historical process of revelation, at the heart of what we are studying: "By a secret and wise disposition of Providence, this blessed Spouse of the Virgin Mary, guardian and provider of the Incarnate Word, has remained hidden from the eyes of man for long centuries and has thus been deprived of veneration and honor. But at the times set by him, God has raised illustrious heralds to proclaim the great attributes of this holy Patriarch and to spread his cult." Then came a few names, then came Pius IX. With the coming of such a pastor, "testimonies of a most loving and ardent devotion," at last, were breaking forth everywhere.

On the other hand, authors thought that Joseph had an eminent role to play in the Church, especially "to appease hatreds and revolts, to restore the true peace."

Moreover, he must "give joy to the Church and nourish it with gifts from heaven, watch over and defend this Mystical Body of Christ." He would then be doing what he had done in the days of

Jesus Christ, the same operation since, as the council points out, "by his ministry he is raised to the order of hypostatic union" (that is, he belongs, as Suarez used to say in the sixteenth century, to the mystery of the incarnation).

The text concluded with a vibrant address, exhorting the pastors to promote his cult, and with a most beautiful prayer. The overall effect was particularly overwhelming. A breath of the Spirit swept over the assembly.

A glance at the Congregations claiming to be of St. Joseph also speaks for itself: the founders are often outstanding women possessing firm qualities which remind us of St. Teresa of Avila. They are, for instance, Emily of Vialar whose Congregation was particularly pleasing to God, according to the Curé of Ars, Emily de Rodat, Anne-Marie Javouhey of whom King Louis-Philippe said: "Mother Javouhey is a great man!" Their Congregations were to exercise an influence throughout the whole world.

There were also founders like Pierre-Bienvenu Noailles, a man of peace, courage and flexibility, and his Society of the Holy Family of Bordeaux. He wrote to his spiritual daughters: ". . . as much as it is possible for simple creatures to be like such perfect models, be gentle and merciful, obedient like Joseph; be humble, modest and pure like Mary; be poor, industrious and faithful like St. Joseph; worthy children of the Holy Family, be of one spirit with it, of one heart."[22]

Even without going into details, one cannot help but see a common trait in all these foundations: they happily bring a sense of concrete detail together with an intense union with God. Jeanne Jugan's Little Sisters of the Poor are a true illustration of this union achieved between "the lowly and the sublime," of which Péguy spoke better than anyone else; this union is, as it were, the stamp of St. Joseph's world.

Sorrowful Times

In his decree *urbi et orbi* of December 8, 1870, officially proclaiming St. Joseph as the patron saint of the universal Church, Pius IX alluded "to the sorrowful times" the Church was going through; having recourse to such a protector was all the more justified. Three months prior to this proclamation, the Piedmontese troops had invaded the Papal States. The pope was being held prisoner in the Vatican. A whole world was definitely falling apart. St. Joseph was called upon by the events themselves to play his role of "Patron Saint of a Happy Death," that is of being the indispensable expert in the trying moments of human existence.

In truth, this episode was just one more in a long series of trials: at the very beginning of his pontificate, the pope had to go into exile in Gaeta and bear the assaults of all kinds of hostile forces at work in Italy and elsewhere. Anticlerical liberalism, freemasonry, the endorsed decisions of Catholics in several countries and especially in France, the extremely strong political ferment everywhere, the rise of nationalism, all this was contributing to make these times most difficult for the Sovereign Pontiff. His response was the Bull *Quanta Cura* and the *Syllabus*, condemning eighty-four errors in vogue (1864).

At the same time, never had the papacy been so exalted, so influential: "Papacy is no longer a thesis in theology," said Vanon Jarry. The more numerous the trials the head of the Church had to face, the more his devotion to St. Joseph grew. Moreover, in a similar movement, popular fervor vested the Vicar of Christ with an importance he had never had in history. The acknowledgment of papal infallibility was to be, as it were, the historical path along which the papal function was to be promoted.

Let us go back again to the writer E. Hello, forgotten today, but whose well-advised contemporaries, like the Curé of Ars, considered to be a superior mind: "The nineteenth century speaks, weeps, cries out, boasts, despairs, displays something of every-

thing; it detests private confession but breaks out into public confessions at every moment. It exaggerates, roars. Ah well! Such will
be this century, this century of uproar, which will see the glory of
St. Joseph rise in the heavens of the Church. St. Joseph has just
been officially chosen to be the patron saint of the Church during
the raging storm. He is better known, prayed more, and more
venerated than in the past. In the midst of thunder and lightning, the
revelation of his silence imperceptibly makes its way,''[23]

One must acknowledge that Pius IX's pontificate is, as it were,
invisibly accompanied by the growing presence of St. Joseph.
There is nothing surprising in the fact that the Sovereign Pontiff
affirmed on February 2, 1878 during his last audience, five days
before he died, to a religious who was filled with admiration for his
serenity: ''Ah! That comes from the fact that today St. Joseph is
better known. I am expressing my trust. If I am not, my successor
will be the one to witness the triumph of this Church of which I
officially chose him to be the patron saint.''[24] Contemporaries,
endowed with shrewd minds, like Monsignor Pie, Bishop of
Poitiers, pondered over the development, then so new, of the cult
of St. Joseph: ''The cult of St. Joseph was one of these gifts that the
head of the family, a wise steward, had intended to draw from his
treasure at a later date; it was one of these reserves and, one could
say, one of these surprises that the supreme master of ceremonies
of the feast of the souls had saved for the end of the banquet. . . .''[25]

A Follow-Up Is In The Making

Barely a few months before Pius IX was elected pope, there
was born in a modest family in Canada, a land traditionally belong-
ing to Joseph, a particularly puny child, Alfred Bessette, chosen by
divine Providence to orchestrate the efforts of Pius IX in a magnificent way. The great Pontiff and the humble brother worked exactly
at the same task, at the same time, as did a no less humble girl of

Lourdes, the exact contemporary of this little Canadian. Bernadette and the one who would become the famous Brother André were of the same height (1.40 m), of the same age except for a few months, suffered in the same way from poor health, poverty, a total absence of human means and had the same success in their astonishing mission! One will be at the origin of the largest shrine in the world built in honor of Mary; the other at the Oratory of St. Joseph, the largest Catholic church, second only to St. Peter's in Rome.

On both sides of the Atlantic, their destinies met in the same month of August 1872 when the poor Brother, useless and scorned, was admitted at last into the Congregation of the Fathers of the Holy Cross dedicated to St. Joseph, while the young girl from Lourdes, who had become a Sister of Nevers, found in St. Joseph the father to replace the cherished François Soubirous who had died the previous year, three months after December 8, 1870.

On November 19, 1954, Cardinal Léger recalled the unexpected developments of the story of Brother André and of his Oratory. Bernadette had requested on behalf of the Lady that a chapel be built ("even if very small . . ." she had added on her own in her excitement); similarly the humble Brother had felt impelled to put up a minute construction in honor of St. Joseph in 1904. Fifty years later, a gigantic church had replaced it. Brother André died on the feast of the Epiphany in 1937 and the proceedings for his beatification were begun almost immediately. From the sole human point of view, "this work would have appeared to be totally absurd," said the Cardinal, "but willed by God, erected by him, led by him, it became possible. What men considered to be folly, God accomplished in this place and in what an admirable way! 'Unless the Lord builds the house, those who build it labor in vain' (Ps 127:1). It is God, one could even say, God alone who built this sanctuary on the mountain; God is the one who made it grow and he is the one who will guide it to its fulfilment. There is not one stone in this building that does not highly testify to the fact that it is there only because God wanted it there. When one sees this amazing spectacle, one understands how Jesus could reply to the Pharisees who were protesting against the acclamations of the crowd: 'If these were silent, the stones would shout out' (Lk 19:40). Here the crowds did not remain silent, but the stones themselves joined with the crowds to sing the glory of God and his goodness and to proclaim at the same time the great attributes of St. Joseph.' "[26]

When Brother André died on January 6, 1937, in spite of the cold weather and the snow, about one million people went to the Oratory of St. Joseph of Mont-Royal to pay their last respects to him. Pilgrims were flocking in from Canada, from the United States and, day and night, this crowd was pressing forward against the doors of the shrine. One had to wait for hours before reaching the tiny wooden casket and see for the last time this little wisp of a man who had helped and healed thousands of his brothers throughout his long life.

ANNEX: *THE REVELATION OF*
ST. JOSEPH'S GLORY

Here is how an Italian Dominican, Isidore Isolani, at the beginning of the sixteenth century, at the very moment when St. Teresa of Avila was born, was proclaiming the revelation of the mystery of St. Joseph.

"The Lord, in order to honor his name, decided to make St. Joseph the leader and the patron saint of the militant Church. Before the day of judgment all the peoples will know and revere the name of the Lord, and the magnificent gifts that God has given St. Joseph, gifts he has wanted to keep almost hidden for a long period of time. It is then that the name of Joseph will abound with all the goods of the earth. Churches will be built in his honor. Peoples will celebrate his feasts and will make solemn promises to him. For the Lord will open the ears of their intelligence and great men will scrutinize the inner gifts of God hidden in St. Joseph and will discover a precious treasure such as we do not find its like in any of the fathers of the Old Testament. This will happen especially through the enlightenments given by the holy angels. St. Joseph will give graces from heaven on high to people who will invoke him, and he himself, constantly surrounded with the majesty of his glory, will borrow nothing from any mortal. The name of St. Joseph will be honorably placed on the calendar of the saints and he will no longer be the last; for a main feast will be set to venerate him. The Vicar of Christ on earth, prompted by the Holy Spirit, will rule that the feast of the foster-father of Christ and of the husband of the Queen of the world, be celebrated throughout the Church.''[27]

1 J. Galot, *Découvrir le Père*, Sintal, 1985, p. 198. (English tr., *Abba Father*, Alba House, New York, 1992.)
2 *Premier Panegyrique de Saint Joseph*, (1656, 3rd point).
3 Cardinal Journet, *L'Église du Verbe Incarné*, DDB, 1969, Vol. 3, p. 265.
4 This text from St. John is not about the relationships between the Father and the Son but about Jesus' state of lowliness during the Passion and the glorification he will receive from the Father.
5 ''. . . a kind of impaired caretaker whose flaccid baldness would more aptly don the smoking cap than wear a halo'' (Paul Claudel).
6 There is the encyclical of Pius XI, *Casti connubii* (1930), followed by the teachings of his successors.
7 On this theme, Canon Caffarel has written a beautiful book which clearly traces the progress realized in Christian thought, *Prends chez toi Marie ton épouse*, Feu Nouveau Ed., 1983.
8 Paul VI to 'Equipes Notre Dame' on May 4, 1970, in *L'Osservatore Romano*, Eng. ed., 'The Family, a school of holiness,' May 14, 1970, p. 9.
9 The Second Homily 'Super Missus' in *Saint Bernard et Notre Dame*, DDB, 1953, pp. 107-108.
10 Those who might be interested in the details of this history should refer to the *Cahieres de Joséphologie*, Center of documentation in Montreal.
11 *Cahiers de Joséphologie*, Vol. 2, July 1953, pp. 186-187.
12 Msgr. Villepelet, *Les plus beaux textes sur saint Joseph*, La Colombe, 1959.
13 *The complete works of St. Teresa of Jesus*, 3 vols. trans. and edited by E. Allison Peers, Sheed & Ward, London, 1950, vol. 1, *Life*, ch. 6, pp. 34-35.

14 Ibid., p. 36.
15 "I thought that Our Lady suddenly took me by the hands and told me I was giving her great pleasure by serving the glorious St. Joseph"; ibid., *Life*, ch. 33, p. 230.
16 One important volume of the *Cahiers de Joséphologie* is devoted to the presence of St. Joseph in the sixteenth century. Another yet more important one, vol. 35, appeared in 1987. It is devoted to the presence of Joseph in the seventeenth century and was the topic studied at the international gathering held at Kalisz in Poland in 1985. This remarkable work shows in a striking way the importance of St. Joseph in the Europe and America of the seventeenth century, both influenced to a large extent by the Carmel.
17 Leonard of Porto Maurizio, *Sermons*, Casterman, 1858, p. 24.
18 St. Alphonsus Liguori, *Une année de méditations*, Avon, 1887, p. 581.
19 E. Hello, *Physionomie des saints*, Palmé, 1875, St. Joseph.
20 *Estudios Josefinos*, p. 27 (1973), pp. 3-39, pp. 170-197. Cf T. Stramare and his well-documented work, *San Giuseppe nella Sacra Scrittura, nella teologia e nel culto*, Piemme, Rome, 1983.
21 *Acta conciliorum*, Collectio Lacensis, vol. 6, col. 847.
22 Preface to the Rule of 1851. Cf Flanagan, *In His Steps*, Apost. of Editions, 1981, p. 91. There are, in the nineteenth century, as many as sixty-one Congregations each claiming to belong to St. Joseph.
23 E. Hello, op. cit., p. 139.
24 A. Ricard, *Saint Joseph, sa vie et son culte*, Lille, 1892, p. 327.
25 Msgr. Pie, *Oeuvres*, Paris, 1886, vol. 7, p. 117.
26 Msgr. Villepelet, op. cit., p. 243.
27 *Somma dei doni di San Giuseppe* (1522).

CHAPTER II

The Great Intuitions

1. AN ASTONISHING CENTURY

THE DEVELOPMENT of a coherent thought on St. Joseph and the emergence of his importance took a new turn with the accession of Pius IX to the Holy See, as we have just seen. But anything we will ever be able to affirm about him in the future will, surprisingly, have already been foreseen in the seventeenth century. In more precise terms, the Holy Spirit had worked in this sense in a particular, but hidden away, between 1560 and 1660.

It was in 1560 that Teresa of Avila, at the age of forty-five, experienced a profound desire to reform the Carmel, an initiative which was to culminate two years later in the creation of the St. Joseph of Avila Convent.

On June 7, 1660, the young Spanish infanta crossed the Bidassoa on the arm of the royal heir to the French throne whom she was to marry two days later in St. Jean de Luz. This young queen was to play a direct role in the consecration of France to St. Joseph, on March 19, 1661, a day of rejoicing throughout the whole kingdom and highlighted by Bossuet's second panegyric, a true monument to the glory of our saint.

On this same June 7, 1660, St. Joseph appeared on the slopes of Mont-Bessillon in Provence to give some water to an unfortunate shepherd boy dying of thirst. This is one of the rare apparitions of this man, so unobtrusive although so present. The symbolism is eloquent: "I am Joseph, lift the rock and you will drink." The rock was so heavy that the shepherd hesitated. The order was repeated. The shepherd boy attempted to move it: the rock toppled over easily and water gushed forth. This is simply a biblical symbol: "He made water flow for them from the rock . . ." (Is 48:21).

St. Paul would meditate on this "spiritual rock," the source of living water which accompanied the Hebrews in the desert: "and the rock was Christ." (1 Cor 10:4).

Everything comes to us through Christ, he is our unique treasure and there our heart must be. But this treasure is given to us by the one inseparable couple, Mary and Joseph. The Lord will use this interplay of symbolic images again in Lourdes. Here on Mont-Verdaille at Cotignac, Mary had preceded her husband by appearing in 1519 on August 10 and 11: this was the origin of the pilgrimage to Our Lady of Graces, which was well known in the sixteenth century. The devotion to Our Lady of Graces was directly linked with the eagerly anticipated birth of King Louis XIV who was to go there himself in thanksgiving on February 21, 1660. And so it was in this same year that Joseph in turn showed himself on the slightly more elevated Mont-Bessillon. The site is enchanting, the view extends far and wide. Mary thus introduces Joseph who then gives a new prominence to the mystery of Mary. This is the very grace of Nazareth, the grace of the incarnation that the seventeenth century probed more profoundly than the others.

Between 1560 and 1660, three protagonists played a decisive role for the subject which concerns us: St. Teresa of Avila, St. Francis de Sales and Jean-Jacques Olier.

St. Teresa (the first daughter of Joseph in history) showed the amazing value of this spiritual kinship. Her foundations and her works were particularly eloquent. The works were translated into French in 1601. They were shocking for some because of the love Teresa expressed toward Jesus and the emphasis she gave to the humanity of Christ. They amazed others and, in a very special way, the well-bred social group which met on *rue des Juifs* at the home of Madame Acarie, a woman of great worth. It is there that Francis de Sales, the future bishop of Geneva, came to know the great Spanish lady. He worked energetically for the installation of the first Carmelite sisters who came from Spain. Teresa's Carmel gained a foothold in France on October 15, 1606 and, in spite of difficulties, it would see an incredible expansion in France and Belgium.

St. Francis de Sales, like St. Teresa of Avila, was to become an exceptional disciple of Christ and a perfect lover of divine Wisdom. As for Joseph, it is difficult to love and revere him more than Francis did: he admitted that Joseph was the "saint of our heart, the father of my life and of my love."[1]

Everything happened as if St. Francis de Sales, just before his death in Lyon on December 28, 1622, was directly introducing the third protagonist of this revelation of Joseph, Jean-Jacques Olier.

In 1622, Jean-Jacques Olier was fourteen years old. His mother, née Séguier, one of the most prominent families of France in the seventeenth century, was despairing of this turbulent boy who was as insensitive to warnings as to punishments. She had brought him to the famous bishop whom Monsieur Olier, the father, an administrator for the province, had at one time thought of lodging in his home. The saint had clasped the young boy in his arms, had hugged him, had blessed him and had said to his astonished mother: "He will be a great servant of the Church!" This blessing, like that of the patriarchs, of Isaac blessing Jacob, Joseph's father, undoubtedly conveyed a secret! The fact is that no one to this day would have insights into the mystery of Joseph as penetrating as those of Monsieur Olier. He died, pastor of St. Sulpice, in 1657.

A fourth man, an outstanding contemporary, St. John Eudes, as we shall see, had also had a glimpse of the secret keys to the mystery. Monsieur Olier held him in the highest esteem and called him "the rare object of his century."

2. *ST. JOSEPH OF AVILA*

In 1560, Teresa of Avila was forty-five years old. She was a religious in the large Convent of the Incarnation but she felt inwardly impelled to create something else. She was apprehensive for she could foresee the objections others would not fail to raise: let her begin by reforming herself! Are there not things to change where she is, without creating something else? She knew she was running the risk of being denounced to the Inquisition, of being exposed to humiliating public penances, of even being sent to prison for life. A house without a revenue does not stand to reason by human standards. Are not hypocrisy, pride, delusions of grandeur, the source of all this? Besides, she was making up all these objections herself and the devil was extremely helpful, as she admits. Would she be physically able to bear the austerities she could foresee? "I certainly think this was one of the worst times that I have ever lived."[2]

Meanwhile, the monastery would be founded as Jesus had promised in spite of all the difficulties. We are touching here upon an essential point: one must read chapter 32 of the *Autobiography* attentively in order to detect a message in its very structure.

The chapter begins with a rather unforgettable description of hell of which the Lord had given Teresa a glimpse in 1559. A place utterly hideous "where there is nothing left to love." Neither devils nor flames. A total absence of beauty, the atrocious tortures of anguish, of darkness, of suffocation and, especially, a horrible despair of heart. Years later, she would still shudder at the thought. "I repeat, then, that this vision was one of the most signal favors which the Lord has bestowed upon me; it has been of the greatest benefit to me, both in taking from me all fear of the tribulations and disappointments of this life and also in strengthening me to suffer them."[3]

Indeed, many people touch the boundaries of this hell, a place where love is impossible, a condition worse than death for a soul essentially made to love.

This vision, in this same chapter 32, helped to define this world, about to come into being on August 24, 1562, as the exact antithesis of hell: the first Reformed Carmel, the Convent of St. Joseph of Avila. A little Holy Family on earth! This little convent was as God wished it to be, according to a description Jesus gave her one day after communion. He wanted it to be dedicated to St. Joseph. He explained that Joseph "would watch over us at one door and Our Lady at the other; that Christ would go with us; that the convent would be a star giving out the most brilliant light."[4]

All is said here: this world of God, the antithesis of hell, is Joseph's world. It has two doors: the first, the entrance door, the one on the street, is entrusted to Joseph. It allows one to leave a complicated, confused, hostile and dangerous world behind. The other is the mysterious door, Mary's door, that ancient devotion called "Gate of Heaven," through which Jesus enters into the world, in a very special way. Everything happens as if the Lord were presenting himself between these two doors in the same way that the eternal Father presents himself, according to St. Irenaeus, between "his two hands which are the Son and the Spirit." The Son imitates the Father: he also has two hands: Joseph by whom he pulls us away from this ambiguous world, this Babylon where people think they all speak the same language while no one understands his brother and Mary, by whom the Son inaugurates the new world, that of Pentecost, where each one speaks his own language, is respected in his uniqueness, but where everyone understands everyone else! We must go through the first door so that the Spirit of the Father who comes through the second might reveal the Son to us (cf Lk 10:22): "No one comprehends what is truly God's except the Spirit of God" (1 Cor 2:11).

The Carmel* was founded. Its beginnings were very humble

---

* Foundation for Discalced Carmelite nuns. The First Discalced Carmelite Monastery, founded by Teresa on August 24, 1562, consisted of a community of four.

but controversial. Everything seemed to be unleashed against it. Hell and the world, in the sense used by St. John, could neither understand nor accept an organism so little like them.[5] One is struck by the spiritual stamina of those unfortunate sisters, holding fast, in peace, against a whole city. Five years later, as Jesus had promised, the star was shining with such splendor that the Master General of the Carmelite monks, as well as the bishop, were filled with admiration. Teresa was given all the permissions and the incentives necessary to found other similar convents, for men and for women.

And so it happened that an outstanding man, beyond any doubt a genius among the great ones that have walked this earth, as much for the depth of his mind and his artistic gifts as for his discerning holiness, John of the Cross, would be thrown into the race by the one whom everybody now referred to as the *Madre*. She was fifty-two and he twenty-four. No one was to describe so perfectly the art, difficult in its simplicity, of becoming a "son of Joseph," as Jesus had chosen to remain at the great turning point of his twelfth year.

Indeed, as one reflects upon this, one sees that these rare and striking works, the *Ascent of Mount Carmel* and the *Dark Night of the Soul*, are but the most precise description, the most irreplaceable one there is of the descent from Jerusalem to Nazareth. John of the Cross places his genius and his holiness at the service of this transfer of human reason, much challenged by the snares and the enticements of the world, to this totally different world of faith. In other words, he teaches, with the authority of a master, the art of entering into Joseph's home in Nazareth.

A surprising fact is that a mind as penetrating as his does not seem to have sensed the importance of St. Joseph, as St. Teresa of Avila did. This insight would be given to him only at the end of his life when he was prior in Grenada. One day, because he was unable to go out and hear the confessions of the Carmelite nuns, he sent two fathers in his place. Once they were on the street, they met a man of venerable appearance who spoke to them of the Order in such terms that they were stunned. As for St. John of the Cross, he understood straightaway: "St. Joseph is the one you met! But he did not come for you, he came for me. I did not understand him well enough but that will change."[6]

Actually, without directly referring to him, no one has spoken better of St. Joseph than St. John of the Cross. I personally rely on him as the surest guide in this dark world of faith which he knows better than anyone. There lies the triumph of God's sense of humor!

Those who are pleasing to God are not the ones who cry out: "Lord, Lord . . ." but those who do the will of the Father. St. John of the Cross is, within the Church of God, one of those who introduced the mystery of St. Joseph; beyond any doubt, he is the one who speaks with the greatest authority.

3. A RADICAL INNOVATION

It is difficult to assess the extent to which the arrival of the Carmelites in Paris in October 1604 was a radical innovation. The works of St. Teresa had been translated in 1601: they had been the subject of lively debates. Some cried shame upon her: "This woman is deranged!" they said; "These visions are delirious, this way of speaking of Christ totally immodest!"

Others were overwhelmed: "What simplicity, what power, what realism in love!"

At the heart of the debate, was this rediscovery of the incarnation of the Infant Jesus, of Mary, of Joseph, as living human beings, with whom one could speak on familiar terms, who answered you, who were interested in you. This vision so near, both so profoundly attractive and powerful, of Christ with this unforgettable gaze that Teresa had so often met and which brought her to do such great things, this Christ whom one could love so passionately, like a spouse, during a perfectly marked out spiritual journey: all that was a source of wonder and rightly so.

What about the astonishment caused by these famous Spanish Carmelites who had been fetched from so far? They were poles apart from the common run of religious women. They seemed to mix everything together: prayer, study, work, recreation. They brought their work with them to the chapel, would casually converse with the Lord. The expedition was led by an extraordinary woman, Anne of Jesus, St. Teresa's favorite daughter for whom, in the past, at Beas in Andalusia, St. John of the Cross had composed the *Spiritual Canticle*. She had a deep love for St. Joseph; he had appeared to her several times. It was with him that she had founded important monasteries in Spain. It was with him that she was undertaking the difficult venture of the French foundation. He was the one who should have given his name to the new convent in Paris, right beside St. James' — but Bérulle had refused. Only the next two foundations, Pontoise and Dijon, would bear the name of St. Joseph.[7]

At the beginning of the seventeenth century, France, a country brought to peace by Henry IV, was discovering a completely new way of living one's faith. The success was overwhelming: Carmelite convents were founded everywhere, vocations of top quality were kept busy. Rarely would France know such fervor and such exceptional saints as in this first half of the seventeenth century.

But, unfortunately, contradictions and misunderstandings are the lot of human works.

In contrast to the mystical realism of the Carmelites, there was in France, at this time, a very different current of thought in the Church, what could be called the abstract current. The road to God was presented in esoteric and intellectual abstract terms. Man was called to experience an inner void, a self-surrender, explained in words that were not always clear, where notions of illuminations and self-annihilation recurred, possibly leading to confusion.[8]

This current has always existed in the Church. There is a

temptation in the heart of man, on the one hand, to want to be like an angel and, on the other, to appropriate truths for himself as if these were kept exclusively for the initiates. It is the temptation of the gurus of yesterday and today. St. Irenaeus, Bishop of Lyons in the second century, was already fighting against this dangerous mentality which mixed Christian thought with all sorts of eccentricities borrowed from philosophy or mythology, making the gullible think they were superior beings or turning them into daydreamers.

We well understand this twofold danger in the midst of which we are constantly moving: being too earthbound, making one's god out of one's stomach, as St. Paul says; confining ourselves within the realities of this world as if they were the only ones that exist. "Those who are unspiritual do not receive the gifts of God's Spirit, for they are foolishness to them" (1 Cor 2:14).

Or to be, on the contrary, a daydreamer. To take the excuse of misunderstood devotion, of the illusions of falsified charity, so as not to see the conflicts, the confrontations, the urgent necessities in a harsh world.

In one of his most beautiful texts, Péguy said that "the second difficulty is much more serious than the first, and it is much more subtle, much more hidden, and it easily creates an illusion in beautiful souls, in those who wish to rise and serve."[9]

And one detects traces of this spirit of abstraction in a man as eminent as Pierre de Bérulle, in the first years of his career. He was a priest of great worth, who played an important role at the levels of both history and spirituality. In 1611, he founded the Oratory of France, copied from that of St. Philip Neri in Italy, and this haven of prayer, study and fraternal life had the best of influences on the Church.

One of his main sources of inspiration was the Carmel. He was to clash with the best Carmelites by wanting to impose his views on them while the latter wished to follow the Spanish way. They ended up by leaving France to start a foundation in Belgium.

In a very particular way, he was the cause of much suffering, no doubt unintentionally, for the admirable woman, Anne of St. Bartholomew, the favorite daughter of St. Teresa. She had been with her dear Mother when she breathed her last in the evening of October 4, 1582. She was the one who had best inherited her spirit and, in a special way, her devotion to St. Joseph.

For Joseph, whom we seem to have left behind, was actually present everywhere: he was the secret architect of this radical innovation, with this self-effacement which is so proper to him. The Carmelites wanted to give his name to their new convent in Paris, an important establishment, the starting point of this fantastic adventure within which, one day, the famous Thérèse of Lisieux would win renown and become even better known than the Mother. Bérulle rejected this name and wanted a more exalted designation, one that would recall the most touching mystery of the Lord: it would be named the Convent of the Incarnation.

The lack of understanding between Bérulle and the Spanish Carmelites reached its critical stage while Anne of St. Bartholomew was prioress at Pontoise. She was profoundly unhappy and had to muster all the strength of her spiritual intelligence and of her virtue so as not to break down completely.[10] This misunderstanding between two eminent souls recalls the painful one existing in the temple between Mary and her Son. Such misunderstandings are no longer possible when one has returned to the Holy Family in Nazareth.

Bérulle himself was to suffer persecution, undergo trials and was to become one of the most profound and most influential minds of the Church. His influence was considerable: it was directly linked with a discovery in greater depths of the mystery of the Incarnate Word. Meanwhile, even if he had an extremely strong devotion to Mary, even if he had an idea of the importance of Joseph, as the notes taken by a woman attending one of his conferences testify, he certainly was not enlightened in the way that his young contemporary, Jean-Jacques Olier, was on the very special role of this saint.[11]

All this shows that, whatever the culture, the good will of a group of human beings or of one person may be, the encounter with Christ's humanity is always a trying and profoundly unsettling, incomprehensible venture. This is clearly seen in the Gospel. After three years, Jesus' closest collaborators, such as Peter, did not understand. This is where, today as yesterday, Mary and Joseph intervene. The strength of the Carmel of St. Teresa is to have mysteriously sensed this humanity, to have lived it in depth and therefore understood it somewhat. That will also be St. Francis de Sales' strength.

4. ST. FRANCIS DE SALES

Few men have suggested to their contemporaries what Christ's humanity could be as much as did St. Francis de Sales, that is, a happy encounter between the most attractive that nature has to offer and a vague something coming from elsewhere, undefinable and yet present.

He personified a unique combination of aristocratic well-being and the perfect courtesy of the humblest; a well-versed knowledge acquired at the best academic sources in Paris and Padua and a true simplicity; a gentle and cheerful understanding yet most rigorously demanding; a rare tenderness for human beings and a total freedom. This last trait was especially intriguing. He himself could not explain it: "There is not a soul in the world, I think, who cherishes more cordially, tenderly and, to say it in good faith, is more loving than I am; for it had pleased God to make my heart so. But, nevertheless, I love independent energetic souls who are not womanish; for this great tenderness confuses the heart, disturbs it and distracts it from the loving contemplative prayer to God, and is an obstacle to perfect resignation and total death to self-love. Whatever is not for God is nothing for us. How can it be that I feel these things, I who am the most affectionate person in the world? Truly, I feel them nevertheless, but how I can adjust all that together is a wonder, for it is my opinion that I love nothing else but God and all the souls for God.''[12]

Henry IV was so fascinated by him that he would have liked to keep this native of Savoy in France and make him a bishop in Paris. As for St. Vincent de Paul, who knew what's what, he said of Francis at the canonization proceedings: ''As I went over his sayings in my mind, I experienced such an admiration for him that I was inclined to view him as the man who has best reproduced the Son of God living on earth.''

What is the secret of all this? Exactly the same as it was for St. Teresa: Mary, with whom he entertained a loving relationship in total trust (a kind of relationship he had learned from his own mother, his ''dear mother'' who was only sixteen years his senior) and Joseph whom Mary had revealed to him. He expresses this secret in increasing depth until his astonishing sermon of March 19, before his death, also referred to as the ''Nineteenth Talk'' in the Visitation edition.

St. Francis de Sales simply was a true son of St. Joseph as St. Teresa had been his daughter. He says so in this note sent on March 19, 1614 to his cherished spiritual daughter St. Jane Frances de Chantal:

Annecy, March 19, 1614

My very dear daughter,

Here are the litanies of the glorious Father of our life and our love.
I thought of sending them to you written in my own hand; but, as
you know, my time is not my own. I have, nevertheless, taken the
time to read them over, to make the proper corrections and add the
accents so that our daughter of the Chastel can chant them more
easily without making any mistakes. But you, my daughter, who
will not be able to sing the praises of this saint of our heart, you
will ponder over them like the Bride, and mumble the words to
yourself; that is, your lips being closed, your heart will be open to
the meditation of the splendors of this Husband of the Queen of the
whole world, named Father of Jesus and his first worshipper next
to his divine Spouse.[13]

There is nothing more to be said. We have but to examine
attentively both the words and the tone.

5. THE SHADOW OF THE HOLY MARRIAGE

Unable to consider again every detail of St. Francis de Sales'
thoughts on St. Joseph,[14] let us go back to the essential points.
This Saint, in addition to being a theologian, understood that St.
Joseph's three titles perfectly interlock: first, he is Mary's husband
and, by the very fact, Jesus' father (Mary simply says so herself, he
notes: "Your father and I have been searching for you. . ."). For
this twofold reason, he is expected to be "a righteous man" to a
supreme degree, that is, to be the one who fulfills the secrets of the
"beginning," the one in whom the Spirit of God can dwell.
First he is Mary's husband, inseparable from his wife (a fact the

Church is far from having integrated into her thought and practice). As soon as our author contemplates Mary, straightaway he sees Joseph beside her. In the beginning of his lifework, the *Treatise on the Love of God*, he invokes the one in whom God takes his delight, for it is to her that this work is dedicated:

"But, O all triumphant Mother! Who can cast his eyes upon thy majesty without seeing at thy right hand him whom for the love of thee thy Son deigned so often to honor with the title of Father, having united him unto thee by the celestial bond of a most virginal marriage, that he might be thy coadjutor and helper in the charge of the direction and education of his divine infancy? O great St. Joseph! Most beloved spouse of the well-beloved Mother, ah! how often hast thou borne in thy arms the love of heaven and earth, while, inflamed with the sweet embraces and kisses of this divine child, thy soul melted away with joy while he tenderly whispered in thy ears (O God, what sweetness!) that thou wast his great friend and his well-beloved father!"[15]

Instinctively, he finds again the very terms used by Ubertino of Casale three centuries before him. This thought dwells in him to such an extent that, when his friend, the future Monsignor Camus, precisely requests that he exercise his episcopal fatherhood by ordaining him a bishop in March 1609, he comes back to his favorite theme: "I find nothing sweeter to my imagination than to see little Jesus in the arms of this great saint, calling him Daddy thousands of times in childlike words and with an absolutely filial and loving heart."[16]

In order to bring everything back to basics, we could say that St. Francis de Sales has understood three things, the first being, as it were, the key to the two others.

This first truth, stunning if there ever was one, on which we shall have to reflect since in fact we live by it, is that Jesus was begotten "in the shadow of the holy marriage" of Joseph and Mary. The work of the Holy Spirit, which traditionally corresponds to this shadow, assumes a concrete form expressly willed by God: Mary must live in Joseph's home. Mary gives birth in the shadow of Joseph. "In order to preserve this purity and this virginity, it was necessary that divine Providence put her in the charge and keeping of a man who was a virgin, and that this Virgin conceive and give birth to this sweet fruit of life, Our Lord, in the shadow of the holy marriage . . . not that Joseph had contributed in any way to this holy and glorious fruit, unless it be by the sole shadow of the marriage. . . . And, even though he had contributed nothing of his, he, nevertheless, had played a great part in this most holy fruit of his holy bride; for she belonged to him and was planted right close to him like a glorious palm tree near her own beloved palm tree, which, according to the design of divine Providence, could not and ought not produce fruit unless it be in his shadow and in his sight."[17] Our entire research and meditation, our entire life should be turned toward this blessed shadow, the only source and secret of Christ's humanity.

The other two discoveries made by St. Francis de Sales stem directly from that one.

Since St. Joseph's shadow is the condition for the beginning of Jesus, it is also the condition for our spiritual beginning. To live within the Holy Family precisely means to find again the concrete demands which correspond to this kinship. It is there and there alone that Christ wants to see us grow spiritually with him:

"In the past, the lamps of the old Temple were placed on golden *fleurs de lis*: Mary and Joseph, a pair without its equal, sacred lilies of incomparable beauty between whom 'the Beloved has gone down to his garden' (Song 6:2) and pastures all his lovers! Alas, if I have any hope that this written word of love might enlighten and set the children of light ablaze (Lk 16:8), where can I better find myself than among your lilies? Lilies among which the Sun of justice, 'a reflection of eternal light, a spotless mirror' (Ws 7:26) has refreshed himself so superbly that he experienced the delights of ineffable love for us."[18] It is there that God came among humans, it is there that he comes in reality, it is there that he wishes to meet us, there that he can love us.

The particular atmosphere of St. Francis de Sales' work, which is that of the equilibrium of opposites, corresponds to what we shall understand as the specialty of the house of Joseph. There, the sublime does not come from humans but from God: "I love simplicity and candor in all things. . . ." We must aim only at this simplicity, in an atmosphere of joy, with a positive outlook. "Let us simply think of doing right today; and when tomorrow comes, it will be called today, and we can think about it then."[19]

The third truth, like a junction which allows a whole canal system to function, is that everything here obeys Joseph. He is in charge of providing the soul with the first and most indispensable of blessings: peace of heart. Without it, nothing is possible. At the age of nineteen, the former student of Paris had undergone an atrocious ordeal; he too had touched hell, like St. Teresa, and thought he would be engulfed in it. Shortly after, the ordeal was coming on again in Padua where the issue of predestination plunged him in anguish: he knew the value of peace. "You know," he would tell his Sisters, the Visitandines, "I have always sought to instil in the uppermost part of your memory, this holy equanimity of the mind as the most necessary and special virtue of religion." Now, where does the peace of the Holy Family come from? From obedience to St. Joseph, this mysterious man who is, as it were, directly connected to the Father.

He is talking about a totally meaningful episode, the flight to Egypt: "Our Lord did not want to govern himself but to let himself be carried wherever and by whomever others wished." As for Our Lady, "the angel does not speak to her . . . she takes no offence because the angel speaks to Joseph. . . . She simply obeys because she knows that God has so ordered; she does not ask why but it is enough for her that God wishes it so and that he takes pleasure in the fact that we submit ourselves without any second thoughts."

"When one is submitted to Joseph as to the eternal Father, the most trying circumstances do not erode the peace and the most unheard-of turnabouts become possible. Let it suffice us to know that God wants us to obey without toying with the idea of assessing those we must obey.'' The Queen of angels herself obeys; it is through Joseph's initiative, ''to whom Our Lady submits herself as to her superior,'' that God speaks to her and he does so ''without ecstasies or raptures or visions or goodness knows what else, the kind of nonsense that we make up in our own minds. . . .''[20]

For St. Francis de Sales, Joseph was the ''deputy-Father of Our Lord, in lieu of the eternal Father who, in whatever concerned the life of Our Lord, did not, as a rule, impose his majesty.''[21] This astonishing wording does not appear in the final edition of the *Treatise* but it corresponds exactly to what he thought, to what he was living in depth. In the day-to-day living, it is by learning the absolutely special art of obeying Joseph (we will gradually have a better idea of what this consists in) that, like Jesus, we fulfil the will of the eternal Father.

Monsieur Olier expresses the same truth with yet greater clarity.

6. MONSIEUR OLIER

At the age of fourteen, Jean-Jacques Olier thus received St. Francis de Sales' blessing just before he died (at the age of fifty-five). According to the latter's prophecy, Jean-Jacques would fulfil his mission to perfection, by being successful there where so many others had failed. He would be the first to open the seminaries requested by the Council of Trent one century earlier. He would guide the spirit of the Church in depth in a direction of which today we must rediscover the exact secret: the art (supremely difficult) of *becoming childlike*, since this is the condition to enter into the kingdom of heaven (Mt 18:3). How are we to do that if not by imitating Jesus by being a child like him, between Joseph and

Mary? This is the profound reason why the St. Sulpice seminary is obviously entrusted to Mary and likewise to Joseph.[22]

Monsieur Olier acknowledged this: others had received all sorts of gifts in the Church while he had received the gift of spiritual childhood. Hence, his own proper genius was a combination of audacity and wisdom operating in an atmosphere of trust and naivety, if I dare say, absolutely unique.

His spiritual director had, as it were, chosen this spirit of childhood for him. His spiritual director was Charles de Condren, one of the most enlightened minds of this century already so rich, the successor of the great Bérulle at the head of the Oratory. He was to die on January 7, 1641. On this Christmas 1640, as he took leave of his dear spiritual son, he said to him: "Take the Infant Jesus as your director." An order which goes much beyond what one might think and which became, as it were, Monsieur Olier's secret.

At this time, he was thirty-two and was undergoing a terrible crisis which was to last eighteen months in all. This priest, the issue of a good family, a pleasant personality, an excellent preacher, had become, in a way difficult to explain, absolutely useless. He was "in a daze," so to speak, his mother would sadly say, unable to speak, hardly able to stand on his feet, losing the most basic reflexes, increasingly becoming a burden for his missionary companions. In 1641, not only did his ordeal suddenly come to an end on the Sunday following the feast of Corpus Christi but he succeeded in opening the first seminary in Vaugirard.

Like St. Francis de Sales, he had left behind the amenities of life associated with a person of means and distinction. He had known the power of friendship with women, but his spiritual director asked him not to accept the office of a bishop. He was going to fulfil this rare vocation about which a young Dominican sister, Mother Angès de Langeac, had spoken to him in most startling circumstances. He was making a retreat in St. Lazare in Paris in 1631 under the direction of St. Vincent de Paul; consequently, in a peculiar vision, he saw this young Dominican sister come in. It was only three years later, during a trip to Langeac not far from the Puy, that he met and identified her, not without stupefaction: ''That is true. You saw me twice in Paris where I appeared to you during your retreat in St. Lazare because I had been ordered to pray for your conversion by the Blessed Virgin, God having destined you to lay down the first foundations of the seminaries in the kingdom of France.''[23] She was to die that same year.

Everything is both simple and extraordinary in Monsieur Olier; such are the specific traits of those who have discovered this narrow gate found by very few, the gate to the house of Nazareth. He, who had begun his clerical life in luxury and amusements at the fair in St. Germain, with coach and footmen, had gradually discovered the total gift of self to God. Totally renewed by the terrible ordeal he had undergone at about the age of thirty, he was then to found the seminaries and transform the worst parish of Paris, St. Sulpice, into the model parish of his century.

7. *MONSIEUR OLIER'S SECRET*

Few human beings, no doubt, have lived the mystery of Joseph as intimately as he did. No one has expressed it in such depth. The Church can only repeat what he said inasmuch as the Spirit will allow her to, for one must always, as St. John of the Cross says, ''follow one's reason,'' and consequently this reason must be enlightened. God only slowly reveals the role he has entrusted to the carpenter of Nazareth as if this revelation was to be made with the greatest precautions. No one may see Joseph before it is time and nothing in the world can give direct access to him. As far as Monsieur Olier was concerned, he was fully introduced to him.

As in the case of St. Francis de Sales, we can provide only a few leads, being very much aware that while it is one thing to recopy or to read a sentence, it is something else to grasp its full significance. Monsieur Olier was, quite frequently, not at all well understood neither in his day nor later; somewhat like that charming eccentric character of the thirteenth century, Father Hermann,[24] a Premonstratensian, who had received the name of Joseph because of his spiritual betrothal with the Virgin Mary.

Whatever that may mean, the key to understanding Joseph for St. Hermann Joseph, for Monsieur Olier and for ourselves, lies in Mary. Monsieur Olier was on truly astonishing terms of intimacy with her. He admits he was able to speak of this with an ease at which he was the first to be amazed. One day, when one of his confreres approached him on this subject, he was seized by this outburst of enthusiasm: "I described you to him so naively and powerfully that he was touched and I still more so. . . ."[25] Mary was the one who had inspired Agnès de Langeac about him; Mary was the one who showed him at Notre Dame, the plan for the future seminary, where each seminarian was to have his own small private room, in contrast with what was practiced by St. Charles Borromeo. Besides, he had been much embarrassed by this project and had asked Our Lady to find someone else to direct such a costly enterprise. No, he was really the one Mary wanted and she would make everything work out successfully.

Let us be frank: without Mary, everything Monsieur Olier says about St. Joseph becomes incomprehensible and we run two risks. Either we imagine that we "understand" the bewildering thought he proposes to us, something surprising in itself; or we reject it as absurd, something which would be agonizing (for us in the first place). With Mary, we gradually enter into these dark and necessary insights, for she perfectly safeguards the order of things. She is Christ's masterpiece of grace; Joseph is, as it were, the masterpiece of her love. Through her and in her, the Father and the Son find each other again in Joseph.

No one has more aptly expressed this wonder than the Norman St. John Eudes, a saint of great scope, contemporary with Monsieur Olier and, like him, the founder of seminaries. Let us ponder over the logic, almost mathematical in nature, expressed in his book, *Le Coeur Admirable*: "Yes, next to God. St. Joseph is the first object of the Most Blessed Bride's love and he holds first place in her heart, for Mary being totally given to Joseph as the bride to her husband, the heart of Mary totally belonged to Joseph. . . . It is therefore logical (clear) that Jesus is but of one heart with Mary; as a result, we can say that Mary is but of one heart with Joseph, and Joseph consequently is but of one heart with Jesus and Mary."[26]

With his brilliant genius, St. John Eudes happily expresses what the Holy Spirit can do when he brings about the full interplay of the human, marital, parental, and friendship bonds. Mary gives all she has to her Son. The heart and blood of Jesus come from Mary. With a calm audacity, St. John Eudes contemplates Mary in the heart of Jesus and Jesus in the heart of Mary, as "the heart of his heart . . . the sole principle of all his movements."[27] Joseph, deriving benefit from the unique love Mary has for him, is introduced into this intimacy because in heaven, as St. Bernadette will say some day, there is no jealousy. The Holy Family is already heaven on earth.

There we have precisely Monsieur Olier's secret. He lives by this exceptional quality of human relationships which is the topic of one of Jesus' last supplications before he dies: "That they may all be one. As you, Father, are in me and I am in you, may they also be in us, so that the world may believe that you have sent me" (Jn 17:20).

Monsieur Olier knows where such relationships were lived and where they must be sought.

8. THE MAIN IDEAS

Monsieur Olier's originality, his own grace, is to have detected, along St. Francis de Sales' same line of thought, the perfectly mysterious bond that exists between Joseph and the eternal Father. No one, beyond doubt, perceived this better than he because no one had experienced it; from this experience, he draws a whole new vision of the priestly life.

The most striking text about Joseph is a small booklet found at the end of *La Journée Chrétienne*.[28] Here we are at the core of what has been called the French School of which Monsieur Olier is, according to Brémond, the most illustrious representative at the heart of the Holy Family. This spirituality was to play an eminent role in the Church and in the world.

The main insight is presented straightaway: "The admirable St. Joseph was given to the earth to express the adorable perfection of God the Father in a tangible way. In his person alone, he bore the beauties of God the Father, his purity and love, his wisdom and prudence, his mercy and compassion. One saint alone is destined to represent God the Father while an infinite number of creatures, a multitude of saints are needed to represent Jesus Christ. For the work of the whole Church is solely to give an outward manifestation of the virtues and the perfection of its adorable head and St. Joseph alone represents the eternal Father. . . . Hence, the majestic St. Joseph must be considered as the greatest, the most famous and the most incomprehensible person in the world. The Father, having chosen this saint to make of him his image on earth, gives him along with himself a likeness of his invisible and hidden nature and, in my view, this saint is beyond the state of being understood by the minds of humans. . . ." This amounts to saying that faith alone can detect something there.

Then comes an inimitable elaboration of these ideas: he too thinks, like St. Francis de Sales, that the light illuminating the soul of Joseph was of the same nature as the one illuminating Mary's soul. But, in contrast with other authors, he does not think he should set up degrees, allowing the Mother of God to hold some sort of first place; he grants that Joseph had a kind of beauty and wisdom that knew no limitations since he was Christ's guardian on earth.

And there lies the second principle: "The Son of God, having made himself visible by taking on human flesh, conversed and visibly dealt with God his Father, in the person of St. Joseph, by whom the Father made himself visible to him."

On the one hand, Joseph and Mary are the oratory where Jesus finds the Father again in the Spirit; on the other hand, "the Blessed Virgin and St. Joseph saw the person of God in Jesus."

Like St. Francis de Sales, Monsieur Olier thinks that the Holy Family was a kind of heaven on earth where all the opposites came together. Writing as the spirit moved him, he notes: "There it was a heaven, a paradise on earth, endless delights in this place of grief; it was a glory already begun in the vileness, abjection and lowliness of their life."[29]

"Jesus, I am not surprised that you remained thirty whole years in this house without leaving St. Joseph. I am not surprised that you are inseparable from his person. His house alone is a paradise for you and his house is for you the bosom of your Father from whom you are inseparable and in whom you take your eternal delights. Outside this house, you find only deadly objects, only sinners, these unfortunate causes of your death!"

A short dazzling sentence expresses what no one would dare say or even think: "Jesus saw in him (Joseph) the eternal Father as his Father and the Most Blessed Virgin considered in his person the same eternal Father of whom she was the bride."

The consequences for the Church are clear: if St. Peter was put in charge of the smooth running of the institution, "of its government, its rule and its doctrine," St. Joseph, totally hidden (by contrast to St. Peter who is fully in view) "is established in order to communicate inwardly the supereminent life he receives from the Father and which then flows upon us through Jesus Christ." Every grace, as the Protestants rightly affirm, comes from Jesus Christ alone, but they do not have an adequate clue to the specific role of Mary and, especially, of Joseph in this dialogue between God and humanity.

Like Jesus, we must "tenderly love God the Father in St. Joseph . . . and because in God the Father, St. Joseph is the source of all good and of all mercy, we say of this saint that anything we ask of him we shall obtain."

What is interesting is that priests (who like Joseph, are especially put in charge of the virgin begetting of Christ in souls) should look to him as their model and protector. "And so," he goes on, "we have chosen St. Joseph to be one of the patron saints of the seminary, like the saint in heaven whom Our Lord has entrusted with the express care of priests, according to what he has made known to me through his kindness." Obviously, it is through Mary, the other "patron saint" of the seminary, that Monsieur Olier was aware of these rare wonders.

We will undoubtedly understand better, after all that, how a Jesuit, the exact contemporary of Monsieur Olier, could cry out: "Beautiful sun, father of the day, hasten your course, quickly bring this happy hour into its day, during which all the oracles of the saints must be fulfilled, who promise us that, as we near the end of time, the glories of St. Joseph will be magnificently displayed; who assure us that God himself will draw the curtain and tear the veil that, until now, has kept us from seeing, out in the open, the wonders of the sanctuary of St. Joseph's soul; who predict that the Holy Spirit will constantly operate in the hearts of the faithful to move them to exalt the glory of this divine person."[30]

Monsieur Olier's insights and expressions cannot but be baffling to us. He had warned us of this. Our coming reflections will provide a few glimmers of light.

It is impossible to take leave of the seventeenth century without attempting to hear Bossuet's voice: there is no simpler, more profound text than the third point of the first panegyric of 1656. Besides, the whole sermon was so beautiful that the queen mother wished to hear it again on March 19, 1659, which fell on a Wednesday, and the impression was unforgettable. Bossuet was again chosen by the Court, two years later, on this great

March 19, 1661 when France was consecrated to St. Joseph at the instance of the young queen who had come from Spain the previous year: it was on this occasion that he pronounced these prophetic words: "What is most illustrious in the Church is that which is most hidden."

But let us go back for a short moment to the third point of his first panegyric. There Bossuet meditates on the different vocations in the Scriptures and he notes: "Among all the vocations in the Scriptures, I notice two which seem directly opposite to each other: the first is that of the apostles, the second, that of Joseph. Jesus is revealed to the apostles, Jesus is revealed to Joseph, but with conditions very much in contrast with each other. He is revealed to the apostles in order to be proclaimed by them throughout the universe; he is revealed to Joseph to make him silent and to hide him. The apostles are the lights by which Jesus Christ will be seen by the world; Joseph is a veil to cover him; and under this mysterious veil Mary's virginity and the greatness of the Savior of souls are hidden from our view. Hence, we read in the Scriptures that when people wanted to scorn him: 'Is he not,' they would say, 'the son of Joseph?' So much so that Jesus in the hands of the apostles is a word which must be preached: *Loquimini omnia verba viae hujus*, preach the word of this Gospel; and Jesus in the hands of Joseph is a hidden word: *Verbum absconditum*; and it is not permitted to disclose it. Indeed, see what follows. The divine apostles preach the Gospel so highly that the sound of their preaching echoes up to the heavens. And St. Paul dared to say that the counsels of divine wisdom came to know about the powers of heaven 'through the Church,' says this apostle, and through the ministry of the preachers, *per Ecclesiam*. On the contrary, when Joseph hears of the wonders of Jesus Christ, he listens, admires and keeps silent."

A little further on, he is astounded as he looks upon the obscurity of Nazareth which will later fascinate Charles de Foucauld: "For at last I will not be afraid to say it: My Savior, I know you better on the cross and in the shame of your torture than I do in this lowliness and this hidden life. Your body is all in shreds, your face covered with blood and, far from appearing as a God, you do not even have the figure of man; nevertheless, you are not so hidden from me and, through so many clouds, I see a few rays of your greatness in this constant determination by which you overcome the worst torments. Your suffering has dignity since it makes you find a worshipper in one of the companions who shares your torture. But here I see nothing that is not lowly and, in this state of self-annihilation, an ancient writer is justified in saying that you are abusive to yourself: *Adultus non gestit agnosci, sed contumeliosus insuper sibi est.* He is abusive to himself because he seems to be doing nothing and is useless to the world. But he does not reject this ignominy, he really wants this injury to be added to all the others he has borne, provided that by hiding himself with Joseph and with the blessed Mary, he may teach us by this great example that if some light is brought forth in the world, it will come from the wish to be of benefit to us, and to obey his Father; that, in fact, all greatness consists in conforming ourselves to God's commands, in whatever way he may wish to dispose of us, and finally that this obscurity we fear so much is so illustrious and glorious, that it can be chosen even by a God.''

There is but one thing to do: memorize these texts and recite them to oneself. One never grows weary of them.

ANNEX: *ST. FRANCIS DE SALES AND THE ASSUMPTION OF JOSEPH*

There was no doubt in St. Francis de Sales' mind that St. Joseph is in heaven, body and soul. Any other thought, according to him, should be cast aside. Here is an excerpt from the last sermon he delivered on St. Joseph.

''What is there left for us to say now if not that, in no way must we doubt that this glorious saint enjoys much credit in heaven in the company of the One who favored him so much as to raise him there, body and soul; something which is all the more likely since we have no relic of him here below on earth. It seems to me no one can doubt this truth; for how could he have refused this grace to St. Joseph, he who had been obedient at all times in his entire life?

"Undoubtedly, when Our Lord descended into Limbo, he was reasoned with by Joseph in this way: 'My Lord, please remember that you came from heaven down to the earth, that I welcomed you in my house, in my family, and that as soon as you were born, I took you in my arms. Now that you are going to heaven, take me there with you. I accepted you in my family, now accept me in yours, since you are going there . . . I carried you in my arms, now take me in yours, and since I took care to nourish and guide you in the course of your mortal life, take care to lead me into immortal life.'

"And since it is true that by virtue of the Most Blessed Sacrament our bodies will be raised on the day of Judgment, how could we have doubts about Our Lord raising the glorious St. Joseph up to heaven, body and soul, he who had the honor and the grace of carrying him so often in his holy arms, arms in which Our Lord had found so much delight? O how many kisses did he give Joseph so tenderly with his blessed lips to reward him in some way for his work!

"St. Joseph is therefore in heaven, body and soul, there is no doubt about that. O how happy we shall be if we can be worthy of having a share in his holy intercessions! For nothing will be refused him, neither by Our Lady nor by his glorious Son.

"If we have faith in him he will ensure that we grow in all kinds of virtues, but especially in those we find he possessed to a higher degree, these being holy purity of mind and body, the most lovable virtues of humility, constancy, valor and perseverance, virtues which will make us victorious over our enemies in this life and earn us the grace to enjoy the rewards which are being prepared in eternal life for those who will imitate the example set by St. Joseph in this life; a reward which will be no less than eternal happiness in which we shall enjoy a clear vision of the Father, the Son and the Holy Spirit. Blessed be God!''[31]

1 Cf *L'Anné sainte de la Visitation*, vol. 1, p. 337 (Vives, Paris, 1866), vol. 10, p. 447.

2 *The complete works of St. Teresa of Jesus*, op. cit., vol. 1, *Life*, ch. 36, p. 252.

3 Ibid., ch. 32, p. 217.

4 Ibid., p. 220.

5 Read in the *Vie de sainte Thérèse* by Marcelle Auclair (Seuil, 1950), the details of these terrible ordeals of the first months (pp. 162-169).

6 Cf Father Crisogono of Jesus, *Jean de la Croix*, p. 235. The episode takes place in the convent of Los Martires, between 1582 and 1585.

7 On this fascinating story, read the life of *Anne of Jesus* by Sister Marie Anne of Jesus, Lion de Juda, 1988, pp. 28, 29, 40, 102, 107.

8 An English Capuchin friar, Benedict of Canfeld, published in 1608 his *Rules of Perfection* which give a good illustration of this way. St. Francis de Sales advised against these because they could be misunderstood.

9 *Véronique ou dialogue de l'Histoire avec l'âme charnelle*, La Pléiade, *Oeuvres en prose*, 1909-1914.

10 A Carmelite monk, Father Urquiza, has just published in Rome *Les oeuvres de la Vénérable Anne de Saint Barthélémy*. The scope and depth of this episode stand out clearly in the study of these texts.

11 Dupuy, *Morceaux choisis de Pierre de Bérulle*. H. Brémond, an outstanding expert in this period, is astonished, rightly so, that a mind as penetrating as Bérulle's did not have a greater intimacy with St. Joseph, *Histoire littéraire du sentiment religieux au XVIIe siècle*, vol. 3, p. 98, note 2.

12 Francis de Sales, *Lettres d'amitié spirituelle*, edited by Fr. A. Ravier, DDB, 1980, p. 751.

13 Francis de Sales, *Oeuvres complètes*, Vives, vol. 10, p. 477.

14 These thoughts were the subject of an article on the first publication of the *Cahiers de Joséphologie* in 1888.

15 Francis de Sales, *Treatise on the Love of God*. Trans. Rev. Henry Benedict Mackey, OSB, Westminster, Maryland, 1945. Dedicatory prayer, p. 1.

16 Francis de Sales, *Letter d'amitié spirituelle*, op. cit., p. 502.

17 Francis de Sales, *Oeuvres complètes*, ed. of the Visitandines of Annecy, vol. 6, p. 354.

18 Francis de Sales, *Oeuvres complètes*, La Pléiade, p. 333.

19 Francis de Sales, *Extraits de lettre*, Vitte, 1941, p. 156.

20 Francis de Sales, *Oeuvres complètes*, Annecy ed., op. cit., vol. 6, pp. 38, 44-45.

21 Francis de Sales, *Oeuvres complètes*, La Pléiade, p. 1534.

22 Faillon, *Vie de Monsieur Olier*, 1875, vol. 3, p. 81.

23 Cf the interesting conference on *Mère Agnès de Langeac et son temps*, Le Puy, Dominican Sisters of Mother Agnes, 1986.

24 Cf *Dictionnaire de Spiritualité*, p. 308. He was canonized in 1958.
25 H. Brémond, *Oeuvres complètes*, vol. 3, p. 448.
26 St. John Eudes, *Le Coeur Admirable*, vol. 8, ch. 3.
27 *Ibid.*, book I, ch. 4 and 5.
28 J.J. Olier, *La journée chrétienne*, Roger and Chernoviz, 1906.
29 Vileness comes from the word vile, linked with the idea of scorn, abjection.
30 P. Jacquinot, *Les gloires de Joseph*, Dijon, 1645. Cf. Msgr. Villepelet, *Les plus beaux textes sur saint Joseph*, p. 100.
31 *Oeuvres complètes*, Annecy ed., *op. cit.*, vol. 6, pp. 369-370.

CHAPTER III

Bernadette's Contribution

1. PIUS IX AND BERNADETTE

PIUS IX was aware of the fact that he had played a key role in the revelation of the mystery of St. Joseph. He died comforted, as he said, by the thought that he had succeeded in making the Father's secret better known. Bernadette Soubirous' span of life from January 7, 1844 to April 16, 1876 roughly coincided with the all important pontificate of the one considered to be the first great pope of modern times. She was born a few months before he arrived in Rome and she survived him by a few months. If we set up a "historical" framework, as we do in mathematics, Bernadette is the one who provides a time "frame" for Pius IX.

Nothing apparently indicated that there should be any relation between this pontiff caught up in the upheavals of history, and this sister, the poorest and the most self-effaced person one could imagine. But Mary and then Joseph, in the name of Christ from whom all things come in heaven and on earth, would plan quite the opposite.

What concerns Mary is known. After he had consulted the bishops in the entire world, Pius IX dared proclaim that Mary, by the blood of her Son, had been preserved from all sin, even original sin, from the first moment of her conception. This question, debated for centuries by the greatest minds, came to a conclusion in the proclamation of the dogma on December 8, 1854. On March 25, 1858, Mary assumed her title before Bernadette by using a most unusual wording: "I am the Immaculate Conception," as if she were saying that she was not only "conceived" immaculate, but that she was also "conception." This astounding association between Rome and Lourdes would, one day, on December 17, 1876, be the occasion for the little sister to address a letter to the pope, the true sovereign, although deprived of his State.[1]

What concerns Joseph has never been studied for the simple reason already pointed out in connection with Vatican II, at the beginning of this study: what touches upon Joseph is generally carefully hidden and is of no particular interest. Perhaps someday we will see that this aspect of Bernadette is important: the day Pius IX formulated his great proclamation on the glory of Joseph by declaring him the patron saint of the universal Church was the fourth anniversary of the death of Louise Soubirous, a death which gave Mary to Bernadette as her mother. The death of the much beloved father, François Soubirous, would come three months after the Vatican proclamation, on March 4, 1871, the first Saturday of the month of Joseph. Bernadette, who had been in Nevers for over four years, understood that Joseph had now become her father.

She underwent the profound experience of Jesus on earth: the parents Jesus had loved, whom he had mysteriously obeyed at the time of his decisive choice, at the age of twelve, became her parents.

The pope in Rome and the humble girl of Lourdes come together like the apostle and the prophet, the two pillars of the Church, to show one direction to the Christians, to teach them to read the new signs.[2]

When we observe these signs closely, we see that they culminate in the Holy Family, this Holy Family in which the Word came, in which the Holy Spirit, as St. Irenaeus says became accustomed to live in Jesus as man. During the thirteen years of her life in Nevers, everything happens as if Bernadette was gradually discovering the very secrets which were already inspiring her life in Lourdes without her being yet fully aware of this. The Holy Spirit loves to come between Joseph and Mary, as the Son of God made man also did himself.

2. *THE SPIRIT OF NAZARETH*

Indeed, the first striking aspect in the life of Bernadette and in the facts of Lourdes is the extreme poverty into which the unfortunate family gradually sank. A poverty of the destitute which recalls that of Bethlehem. A poverty we find painful to observe so horrible does it appear to us: Bernadette seemed to breathe the Gospel in this poverty. Money was what terrified her, the touch of it burned her like a red hot iron! Everything was poor in and around her: her family, her health, her knowledge, her means . . . everything was transparent, everything was inhabited by the Spirit of God.

It was in this context that the Lord would suggest two images of fatherhood to this young girl, the eldest of the family, both of which were destined to play a major role in her life: her father François and the rock of Massabielle.

Once we have had a glimpse of François Soubirous, he remains an unforgettable man. Instead of the heiress of the Boly Mill who had been proposed to him, he married her sister, a love marriage. He was an illiterate man instinctively guided by love. He worked hard as a miller but, quite soon, due to various circumstances, he fell into financial difficulties, then into misery. He was forced to take refuge in *Le Cachot* (the dungeon or the jail), in this old prison, judged to be foul and unwholesome; this was the home for his family of six at the time of the apparitions.[3]

In spite of very harsh conditions, of the suspicion awakened by his poverty which would cast him into prison, François steered his course with dignity. His love for his wife and his children (especially for his eldest daughter), his humble faith, the courage of each one of them, were to keep this poor family from falling into beggary and delinquency. Secretly, François was presiding over a household in which this transparent human being, Bernadette, was growing up and whose austere, loving, courageous life suggests what the life of the Mother of God possibly was on earth.

The rock of Massabielle, venerated today by pilgrims from every part of the world, hardly drew any attention in 1858. On the contrary, it was a filthy pig grotto, a kind of refuge, a grazing ground for the township's herd of swine brought there every day by Samson, their keeper. If Bernadette and her two companions went to this ill-famed site, a place for clandestine rendezvous, where the Gave deposits the debris carried by its waters, it was because there, at least, they would not be accused of stealing the wood or bones they would gather.

And so, the Lord was to choose François Soubirous and the rock of Massabielle to accomplish great things.

François was the "beloved father," Bernadette's favorite human being on earth; as we shall see, he was to introduce Bernadette directly into this understanding, so rare, of the mystery of Joseph.

As for the rock, once it was touched by the blast of the first apparition, once it was lit up by the light from heaven, it was, as it were, transfigured: it would become like the biblical paternal symbol of strength, of fidelity, of protection, of the initiation into the mystery it seemed to conceal, like the waters of a spring.

"You are my Father, my God, and the Rock of my salvation!" the psalmist cried out (Ps 89:26). Bernadette would only say, in her letter of July 20, 1866, a few days after her arrival in Nevers, along with her request for prayers: ". . . especially when you go to the Grotto. It is there that you will find me in spirit, bound to the foot of this rock I love so much."

3. HANDS AND FEET

In Lourdes, Mary makes Bernadette enter into the particularly special atmosphere of the Holy Family which is one of poverty, silence, humble labor; but, at the same time, it is one of peace, of joy, of an astonishing fecundity, the atmosphere in which Jesus was guided and educated for a long time in Mary's company.

Everything happened as if Joseph were revealing himself in this mysterious silence which accompanied most of the apparitions. Mary's words were brief and few: Bernadette perceived them not through her ears but in her heart.

She interpreted what she understood at the level of her hands and feet. Witnesses would never grow weary of contemplating Bernadette's gracious countenance: "Who taught you to greet so well?" a teacher asked her. The children from the school would never forget the sign of the Cross Mary had silently taught Bernadette during the first apparition and that she would repeat for them. Similarly, her feet seemed to obey a mysterious force; for example, on February 22 when, out of obedience, she was going to school she suddenly turned about on the spot and hurried down the road to the grotto where, however, the rendezvous with the Lady would not take place.

It was with his hands and his feet that Jesus at twelve, without a word, had expressed the will of the eternal Father, such as he perceived it to be through Mary's remark: "Your father and I were searching for you. . . ." (Lk 2:48).

Bernadette experienced, with intensity, all kinds of gestures to the good understanding of which she would devote her entire life.

The summit of this mysterious monition from the Queen of angels is reached on February 25, 1858 midway through the apparition: it is the ninth apparition out of eighteen, precisely the middle one out of those that Mary had so graciously proposed to the young visionary. There would be only thirteen apparitions during those

fifteen days and the one of February 25 was the seventh one. This
date marked a turning point:[4] Bernadette, so admired until then,
covered herself with mud, dragged herself like a demented child in
this dirty cavern, ate grass, and drank dirty water. "It would
seem," said a witness, "that she was carrying all the afflictions of
the world."

Bernadette, in her own way and with her whole being was
telling the story of the Passion of the Lord. She accepted, on the
fourth attempt, to drink the dirty water she had gathered by scratch-
ing the ground, in the same way that Jesus would drink the chalice
that his Father offered him (Mt 26:42). She was, as it were,
disfigured, ridiculed, like the Son of Man.

But a spring would gush forth on earth as in heaven. The
pilgrimage was about to begin: the faithful would come not so
much out of curiosity but of fervor, as was noticed from this day
on. The great revelation of March 25, the day of the Annunciation,
became possible. On Easter Wednesday, the day of her death,
twenty-one years later, the flame would lick Bernadette's finger for
some time without burning it any more than death would touch her
body.

One hundred days later, on July 16, came the last apparition,
also silent like Joseph, on this feast of Our Lady of Mount Carmel
which ineffably recalled the prophet Elijah, the great prophet of the
Old Testament, the prophet of Mount Carmel. He too had struggled
against sin, more than anyone else and at the risk of his own life.
His silent prayer had inspired the first Carmelite monks on the very
same sites twenty centuries later at the time of the Crusades. Thus
had been born, in the beginning of the thirteenth century, the Order
of the Virgin Mary which, in the sixteenth century, became the
Order of St. Joseph. The apparitions of Lourdes came to an end in
this atmosphere of the Carmel in the same way that they had begun
in a grotto and in a blast of wind, exactly like in the vision of Elijah
being visited by God at Mount Horeb at the heart of his mission.[5]

But this was not the end. Mary would make Bernadette undertake a journey of revelation as she had helped Jesus to do at the age of twelve.

4. THE GREAT SEPARATION

It was on April 4, 1864, after Mass, that Bernadette spoke of her vocation as a sister of Nevers for the first time. She was twenty and had been thinking for some time of giving herself to God. She had first thought of the Carmelites but her health was an obstacle to that. What she wanted, as she clearly stated on the day she took the habit in Nevers on July 29, 1866, was to "be hidden": "I have come here to hide myself."

After her last farewell to her parents, whom she would not see again, as well as to the group of people dear to her, and to the mountains, she left for Nevers in the morning of Wednesday July 4, 1866. She was twenty-two and, on that occasion, she made "the greatest sacrifice of her life," as she would say later. It was really the death of the little kernel of wheat fallen into the ground.

She arrived in Nevers to start her new life on Saturday, July 7, the seventh day of the seventh month, as the Bible would put it. She was to give an account of the apparitions only once, on Sunday the 8th, then she would be forbidden to speak about them. One short scene at the time reveals that this humble heart, so inhabited and directed by these three secrets which were never revealed, was pursuing a hidden journey. A sister caught her making a novena to the Virgin Mary while kneeling in front of a statue of St. Joseph:

"You are having a distraction. . . ."

"The Blessed Virgin and St. Joseph get along perfectly well and in heaven, there is no jealousy. . . ."[6]

Words striking in their simplicity and which bring together at last what God has joined and which we are constantly separating.

She would take up the same idea again, six years later in a letter addressed to Mother Alexandrine Roques on April 3, 1872, in which she would explain that, after devoting the month of St. Joseph to pray for the cure of the Mother General, her prayers had not been answered — then let Mary intervene: "yet, I would not want to hurt St. Joseph's feelings in any way, he whom I love very much, but in heaven no one takes offence!"[7]

Sister Vincent Garros, her compatriot, recalled with what trust she would ask this saint for "the grace to love Jesus and Mary as they want to be loved," as if the Holy Spirit had precisely confided this important secret to her. In fact, at the beginning of her religious life, St. Joseph was first and foremost the "patron of a holy death" according to the classical custom of the time. And that was how she wrote to her sister Marie after Lent as soon as she could on April 16, 1868 to note, belatedly, the birthday of her brother-in-law, Joseph.

"I especially asked St. Joseph to make a fervent Christian out of him. I also asked him for the grace of a holy death for everyone."[9]

Bernadette had just gone through the great pain of parting from her family. The adaptation to this new life was difficult at first. The profound meaning of what she was living would come to light on the occasion of the death of her father, François, on March 4, 1871. With the loss of this person she loved so much, a whole world was definitely disappearing. Her mother had died on December 8, 1866, on the feast of the Immaculate Conception, at the very moment when, for the first time, the vespers of the feast were being sung in the new crypt inaugurated a few months before. She loved her mother very much but her father was "what she cherished most in this world." The whole world of her childhood was disappearing with him and, at the same time, from now on, being the eldest, she was vested with the authority of the dear departed one. She would intervene, often energetically, in family difficulties.

5. THE DISCOVERY

Henceforth, to the great astonishment of her companions who failed to grasp what was going on, Bernadette, Mary's privileged child as people loved to say, was to realize that Joseph was her father. She lived this fact in depth and, gradually, she came to understand this and to say so. In the month of August 1872, when her humble contemporary, Brother André, in the distant land of Canada, was being admitted at last into the congregation dedicated to St. Joseph, she confided, one day, in the infirmary:

"Be very good, I will go and visit my father. . . ."

"Your father?"

"Don't you know that now my father is Joseph?"[10]

Mary gives her a glimpse of the secrets she had been in charge of revealing to Jesus, secrets wrapped in silence and darkness. Instead of opposing the one he called "my Father" against the carpenter of Nazareth, Jesus, on the threshold of his conscious adolescence, had to see them both together in the same glance. Instead of feeling that her father had disappeared into the past, Bernadette found him again in Joseph. Henceforth, she would say: "He is my father and the patron saint of a holy death." This association of ideas is simply remarkable. The eminent work of the father is to help us accept a death so irreversibly bound with life. Jesus at twelve, Bernadette at twenty-two, both experienced, thanks to Mary, what could be called "the departure of Abraham" or that of the king's betrothed in Psalm 44, also called to leave her country and the house of her father. And that was taking place in the shadow of Joseph, this astonishing character, as powerful as he is self-effaced, like the Holy Spirit. It is in him that Bernadette had come to hide herself.

Henceforth, Joseph obviously held first place among her heavenly friendships. He was at the head of a trio, for example, to which St. Aloysius Gonzaga and St. Stanislaus Kostka belonged. He was bound especially to the life of the Holy Family which, for

Bernadette, was of prime importance. The Holy Family, along with the Garden of Gethsemani, was, as she says, a place of pure love: "Here below, love cannot be experienced without pain."[11] The two places were in perfect correlation but if, for Jesus, the first was the condition to have the second, for Bernadette (and, therefore, for us), the second is the condition for the first. It is because Christ died on the Cross that we can hope to savor something of the extraordinary Holy Family. Bernadette understood that, for Jesus, the journey goes from the Transfiguration to the Cross, but that the Cross allows us to look toward the Transfiguration.[12]

In her small personal notebook, beginning in October 1873, she confides: "O Mary Immaculate, O glorious Joseph! And you, St. John, beloved disciple of the Divine Heart, teach me the great science of love. . . . What matters if nothing appears outwardly as long as I imitate Jesus, as I am in Mary's womb like Jesus, and I accept with joy the privations, the sufferings, the humiliations as Jesus, Mary and Joseph did for the glory of God."[13]

Through the preachers' words but especially through her intimate experience, she had understood the law of spiritual growth which is, as it were, the specialty of the authority ("what causes to increase") of the master of the Holy Family. "In order that Jesus may increase . . . I must diminish. He will increase inasmuch as I diminish. . . . If I do not diminish, I prevent him from increasing. Increase in me, Jesus, increase as you did in Nazareth!"[14]

Everything is summed up in the stunning words which open the little notebook, like the password of the Holy Family: "What concerns me, no longer interests me. From now on I must belong entirely to God and to God alone, never to myself."[15]

Could this have been foreseen? Bernadette, in her adult years, had the same master in prayer as did St. Teresa of Avila, Doctor of the Church, that is, St. Joseph, the one the Father had chosen to communicate with his own Son and Mary, his Mother: "If anyone cannot find a master to teach him how to pray, let him take this glorious saint as his master and he will not go astray . . ."

(*Life*, ch. 6). "When we do not know how to pray," says Bernadette, "we turn to St. Joseph."[16] And she would spend hours at the back of the garden, in the little chapel dedicated to him. People wondered what she could be doing there — they did not dare ask too many questions: "One prays well in this chapel. Oh! Yes . . . I go every time I can. . . ." This chapel would take her back to the Grotto. It would play a new role in the history we are in the process of deciphering; it would end up by being humorous, so much has Providence taken pleasure in concealing everything.

6. DEATH AND BURIAL

When Bernadette felt that death was coming, exhausted, burdened with physical and spiritual ills as she was, she gathered all her strength to ask "her father" on March 19, 1879 the grace of a holy death. Father Fabre, the convent chaplain, was struck by the strength she could still muster to make this request. She did not pray to be healed or that her suffering may abate, but to have the courage to persevere to the end.

This was to be her last March 19. It fell on a Wednesday. She had always observed the feast of her favorite saint with the greatest devotion: a very small statue and tiny candles, so as to bring out by contrast the extreme greatness of the character: "what is most illustrious in the Church is what is most hidden," Bossuet had said when speaking of Joseph.

The Lord came for her after the most moving and the simplest of agonies on Easter Wednesday, April 16, 1879. The burial had to be postponed, so large was the crowd that wanted to see her for the last time. She would be buried, gloriously, during a ceremony which was like a celebration, on Easter Saturday April 19, one month after the feast of St. Joseph. Again we find the alternate of her departure from Lourdes, between a Wednesday and a Saturday, as if Joseph took charge of her death and Mary of her life. On that day, Bernadette's body was laid to rest in the little chapel dedicated to St. Joseph where she had prayed so much.

Where was she going to be buried? Very quickly, the idea of putting her in the sisters' cemetery was cast aside for she had seen the Blessed Virgin, she was the privileged child of the Immaculate Mary. A place in the garden could be found with the authorization of the mayor of Nevers. But this authorization was slow in coming. A good idea would be to send a delegation to the Ministry of the Interior in Paris but it declared itself unqualified to make such a decision. The mayor of Nevers finally decided to authorize the burial wherever they wished but, meanwhile, the Superior had changed her mind. Why not leave her in the chapel of St. Joseph after all? In May 1879, everything was ready; a vault had been prepared, covered with a beautiful tombstone. It is there that Bernadette's remains were laid.

A few years later, when the Superior General, Marie Thérèse Vauzou, who had been opposed to all initiatives concerning the beatification of Bernadette (''Wait until I am dead!'' she said), died in Lourdes, a commission of inquiry was immediately set up, an initiative favored by influential men of the Church. And thus it happened that the vault was opened, as was the custom, to examine the state of the body. This was in 1909; Bernadette had been buried for thirty years. Everything had decayed except Bernadette's body which could be washed and dressed anew before placing it back again in its resting place for another sixteen years.

Thirty years! The time Jesus had spent hidden in the shadow of Joseph! He had emerged from it so radiant that the first disciples had abandoned John the Baptist, the greatest of the prophets, to follow him straightaway without having witnessed the least sign. People were amazed at the wisdom of the son of the carpenter; during his baptism, the eternal Father had proclaimed him his beloved Son, the object of all his love.

An astonishing fact is that this little chapel which is, as it were, the mysterious counterpart of the grotto in Lourdes, will disappear on the same day. As far as the site of the apparitions is concerned, the grotto collapsed on July 16, feast of Our Lady of Mount Carmel. It was on July 16, 1944 that the little chapel was blown up in a bombing: Bernadette's tombstone, recovered intact a little further off, is all that remains.

Pius XI canonized Bernadette on December 8, 1933, feast of the Immaculate Conception in the year which commemorated the nineteenth century of the Redemption.

7. BERNADETTE'S CONTRIBUTION

What Bernadette definitely contributes is simplicity. A particularly cumbersome and difficult contribution for us to accept, for the complicated people that we are. God is simple and he managed to express this simplicity in an exceptional manner through Bernadette.

She makes us follow a path which is her own, which is the one of Jesus' thirty years of formation: everything begins in the extreme poverty of the manger, in this case of Le Cachot. Angels appear freely, warming the shepherds and allowing the apparition of their Queen to the young girl. The entire world is stirred: the Magi travel; the highest authorities of the country are moved by the event of the apparitions. Jesus makes himself known in the temple through Simeon; doctors sense his greatness during his brief appearance at the age of twelve; Bernadette is acknowledged by the Church as a true visionary; theologians are interested in her.

Then it is the terrible separation: Jesus and Bernadette, warned by Mary through whom the Holy Spirit expresses himself, must leave their respective lands and "the house of their father," like the great callings in the Bible. Both descend into the most obscure darkness with a silent courage, all of which, humanly speaking, is perfectly incomprehensible. "There where intelligence sees no more," says Ruysbroeck, "love goes on and enters. . . ." Where do they both enter? In Joseph's place. It is in his home, like Jesus, that Bernadette finds herself in Nevers. It is in his chapel that she breathes. It is Joseph who keeps watch over his dear little girl against the assaults of the evil one and the morsels of death. It is exactly the course followed by Teresa of Avila three centuries earlier; it is Mary who welcomes Teresa in her revered order. Then, after terrible ordeals, Mary makes her daughter understand that Joseph is the one who saved her from death. She encourages her to love him and thus directly fosters the birth of St. Joseph of Avila.

The Church must make this journey which takes her from the temple she has built for herself to this house that God makes for her, as Nathan promised David (1 Ch 17:10), that is, to true interior life, the life of the Holy Family. A journey which is impossible without this death in Jesus of which Joseph is the expert; he had to undergo this total conversion in order to be Mary's husband and the Child's father.

After a childhood as poor as it was wonderful, interwoven with true love, after the mountains, the Gave, the heaven of the apparitions, Bernadette, the daughter of François and Louise Soubirous, was able to train herself to this death to self that, a little later, Thérèse of the Child Jesus and Elizabeth of the Trinity would know. But who is simpler than she was? Who escapes more perfectly from this desire of finding oneself little again, were it only in one's writings, than Bernadette? "What concerns me no longer interests me, henceforth I must totally belong to God and God alone and not to myself."

Why is Lourdes a kind of wholesome land, a privileged space and time for so many pilgrims coming from the world over, among whom some scarcely believe and others practice their faith very poorly? Why do so many hearts open up to tell the priest what we do not always dare tell ourselves? Why all these discoveries, these encounters, these appeasements, this setting out, often definitive, on one's new way?

Why are the sick, the poor, the royalty here? Why so much devotion to people, so much ingenious charity? Why so much joy?

To be sure, there are the apparitions, the rock, the water, the shrines, the mountains, the trees, the motly crowds, the processions. But above all there is an unknown journey that clearly Mary gets Bernadette to make, that she gets many to make secretly. Mary makes the Christians take the road to the Holy Family, where the Gospel is lived in its plenitude. Lourdes, in her heart, is the land of Joseph, where, as we journey onward through it, we learn what makes us live forever.

Considered in all her dimensions, Bernadette comes to relieve Mary in this very special work we have just described. It is a delicate operation, for many aspects within ourselves protest vigorously against it. To be a member of the Holy Family supposes a faith filled with a childlike trust which goes against the pretensions or apprehensions of human reason alone. How can one understand, on the other hand, the Gospel call to poverty without becoming naive, rash, unrealistic? How can one understand a true Marian devotion? How, in the wake of Bernadette, can the professional or family necessities, or a particular calling be integrated with the radical demands one feels the Gospel is making?

It is here that Bernadette's contribution is most original. No one more than she has fully grasped the sense of her own limitations, of her nothingness, realizing all the while that she was profoundly loved by God and, this is a central point, totally surrounded by Mary and Joseph.

The more we can manage to imitate her on this precise original point, the more easily we will give a concrete form to this spiritual "kinship" and the closer we will come to her experience: that of saints; that of Jesus, carried out to the end of his mission, beyond the worst trials, through the Spirit of love, the Spirit of his Father, his Spirit. The courageous fidelity of Bernadette, so simple, so beautiful, is an incomparable word of God for each of us.

ANNEX: *THE ENTRANCE TO THE SANCTUARY*

In keeping with what we have just said, I would like to draw your attention to the choice, as simple as it was enlightened, of the patron saint for each of the entrances to the sanctuary of Lourdes.

For those who do not know or who have not noticed, we enter the sanctuary of Lourdes by going across the bridge over the Gave and walking through the majestic entrance dedicated to St. Michael, facing the basilica.

In fact, because of the layout of the city and its surroundings, pilgrims generally come in through the side entrance which is more convenient. This is dedicated to St. Joseph, represented with the Infant Jesus in his arms. Many may not notice this.

I am reproducing here an article I published in the *Journal de la Grotte*, on March 19, 1985.

"Why did we give the names St. Michael and St. Joseph to the two entrances to the sanctuary? Those responsible in the past undoubtedly had their own reason. Michael is the head of the angels of whom Mary is the Queen: Joseph is the companion on earth of the Mother of God. For two different reasons, they are intimately associated with the One who chose this site.

"There is, it seems, a much more profound reason that the progressive revelation of the mystery of Joseph (a revelation which is only at its beginnings) will clarify, as it were, experientially: it is the mysterious parallel character of Michael's action and that of Joseph in heaven and on earth.

"Michael's task, so powerful and grandiose, is described in Revelation:

'And war broke out in heaven;
Michael and his angels fought against the dragon.
the dragon and his angels fought back,
but they were defeated,
and there was no longer any place for them in heaven.
The great dragon was thrown down,
that ancient serpent, who is called the Devil and Satan,
the deceiver of the whole world;
he was thrown down to the earth,
and his angels were thrown down with him'

(Rv 12:7-10).

"Joseph's task is exercised not in heaven but on earth, exactly in the same sense, but in ways which seem to be inverted: here, everything is simple, at ground level, common, ordinary, in keeping with human views. He can conceal the incarnation because he himself goes absolutely unnoticed. It is not by challenging evil with might that he will triumph, as did St. Michael, but by slipping away stealthily, by fleeing to Egypt, like the cunning serpent who senses that danger is near, the example Jesus used in his teaching to the disciples (Mt 10:16). Some day, St. John of the Cross will explain in the *Living Flame of Love*, that sometimes we must look like the enemy, assume the shape of the serpent the better to escape him!

"The impregnable fortress, where God the Father will make his beloved Son, his Only One, enter, is the humble abode of this carpenter. It is there that all the angels of God will assemble to serve him, no breath of Satan touching him in any way. And to think that we too, if we wished, could learn to decipher the secrets of these two doors in every moment of our lives; we could then enter at will into this incomparable space!"

---

1 The name Soubirous means "Sovereign."
2 On the signs of Lourdes and their spiritual and pastoral implications, see the excellent book by André Cabes, *Marie, chemin de source vive*, Le Chalet, 1986.

3 Pilgrims are strongly impressed by their visit to the *Grotto*. This place strikes them and God speaks to them there. It is a place for conversion.

4 No one has better understood and explained all the symbols of this apparition than Father Bordes, *Lourdes, sur les pas de Bernadette*, pp. 16-17.

5 Plans were made to build a Carmelite convent on the meadow of the last apparition. It was to open eighteen years later, to the very day, on July 16, 1876.

6 R. Laurentin, *Logia de Bernadette*, vol. 1, p. 142. This invaluable study has collected all the reported words spoken by Bernadette in three volumes.

7 A. Ravier, *Les écrits de saint Bernadette*, p. 296.

8 R. Laurentin, op. cit., vol. 1, p. 379.

9 A. Ravier, op. cit., p. 268.

10 R. Laurentin, op. cit., vol. 1, p. 420.

11 Ibid., p. 345.

12 "If from Mount Tabor one must go to Calvary, from Calvary one must go to Mount Tabor, with Jesus. There one finds a foretaste of heaven. The soul follows but one road, from Golgotha to Mount Tabor. It comes out of Golgotha to find strength and courage at Mount Tabor. Such is that ladder of life." (*Carnet*, 1873).

13 A. Ravier, op. cit., p. 369.

14 Ibid., p. 366.

15 Ibid., p. 343.

16 R. Laurentin, op. cit., vol. 1, p. 379.

CHAPTER IV

The Descent of Jesus

1. MARY'S WISH

ALL we have seen until now is based on the history of spirituality. Slowly, but strongly, the Church assures us of one fact: Joseph is great, God has entrusted him with considerable responsibilities which Pope Pius IX has recognized. At the same time, however, everything very often goes on as if this official recognition had no practical impact: Joseph is practically unknown. But we cannot have any doubts about his action; Teresa of Avila, Monsieur Olier, and Bernadette have given us demonstrations of this.

When we reflect on the facts of Lourdes as we have just done, we acquire a kind of conviction: Mary would want her husband to be better known. She told St. Teresa how her devotion to Joseph was a source of joy for her. She expresses herself in the same way to Monsieur Olier: "The Most Blessed Virgin gave me this great saint as a patron Saint, assuring me that he was the protector of hidden souls and adding these words about him: 'I have nothing dearer to me in heaven and on earth next to my Son.' " For his part, Monsieur Olier acknowledges this: "Joseph is a saint God has wished to keep hidden during his life and of whom he has reserved the inner preoccupations for himself alone, without sharing them with the external cares of the Church, a saint that God has manifested in the bottom of hearts and for whom he himself has inspired veneration in souls.''

In the life of Bernadette, everything goes on as if Mary had secretly made her choice confidante understand, prepared as she was among all others by a radical poverty and the worthy household who brought her to life, the particular importance of the one who must remain hidden. Did Bernadette's three secrets, one of which was the prayer that Mary taught her, point to the Holy Family?

Whatever that may be, Mary in Lourdes and in Nevers opens up an original path through Bernadette herself. But, in the same way that Mary wanted Bernadette to be, as it were, the disturbing prophet of an unknown route, so did the eternal Father want Mary to help Jesus, this Son who is the son of both, to choose also a disconcerting route. This is what St. Luke relates in the scene of the temple in chapter 2 of his Gospel. Let us beg the Lord to enlighten us on these difficult questions.

We are now beginning the fourth stage of our work, we are crossing a threshold. We are leaving the history and the thought of the saints behind and beginning to take our own risks as we follow in Jesus' footsteps. To speak of Christ, especially of the child Christ, is a delicate matter: what did he know, he who was God and man? One thing is certain; he was learning. St. Thomas Aquinas put his whole genius to task and accomplished a monumental work to discover that Jesus was truly learning. Is it not paradoxical to think that, while he was the creator of his parents and the source of their holiness, Jesus had something to receive from them? As for himself, how could he be truly man if he did not increase in years, progressing as the Gospel expressly notes?[1]

If, as I believe, the Virgin Mary really wants us to discover in our times the one she designates as father to Jesus at the important moment of the latter's twelfth year, she must come to our help. ''The Holy Spirit will come upon you'' (Lk 1:35) the angel had promised. May she help us to welcome him!

St. Teresa of Avila prayed to the Holy Spirit at length before she began to write the fourth Mansion of her *Interior Castle*, for reasons that are exactly the same as ours: "for we now begin to touch the supernatural."[2] We are leaving behind our human habits, a familiar domain, and going down to Nazareth. Before the fourth Mansion, man is an adult who makes decisions and accomplishes what he is able to do with the help of God: he progresses and becomes a serious human being, applied, pious, and devout. Then comes a kind of profound trial, a fundamental questioning which seems to make his world collapse. A most disconcerting destabilization — a kind of death!

What follows this is different. The discoveries and the style of prayer are so new that help is absolutely essential: what is certain is that the spiritual fruits, also new, begin to appear. The adult learns to become a child, in the way Jesus invites us to be in the Gospel. This is an aspect of conversion that is such a source of joy for the angels of God.

2. THE DESCENT

Jesus is God's Holy One. He therefore has no need of conversion. However, he wanted to experience the difficulty of making heart-rending choices as if he had to make the decision to choose the will of the Father with his human will.[3]

The first time we see this kind of conflict at work in the life of Jesus is on the occasion of his trip to the temple when he is twelve years old. He had gone up to the temple, in the city of David, his forefather on Joseph's side. In the "house of my Father," as he will say. He was twelve; legally speaking he was on the threshold of his full consciousness, a fact which allowed those in authority to declare him one of theirs, a "Son of the Law" (*bar-mizvah*). Jesus is preparing himself fully to assume his responsibilities. But a gripping event takes place and what we have studied above allows us, it seems, to understand him better.[4]

Jesus knows he is the son of the eternal Father. He knows he is the son of the Virgin Mary. He knows that this woman is inhabited by the Spirit who dwells in him in plenitude.

He knows too that Joseph has played the role of a father: it is from him that he has received the twofold nourishment which has allowed him to increase: the bread of man and the Word of God, for which the father was responsible in a Jewish family. These are the bread and the Word spoken of in the ancient text of Deuteronomy (chapter 8) that Jesus will one day set against the tempter in the desert: the profound nourishment of the human being, the daily bread that comes from the Father.

Joseph is the one in charge of this twofold bread, as well as of the human insertion of Jesus in the family of the kings of Judah: it is through him that Jesus is the son of David. Joseph is the one in charge of conveying the fatherly love of the Almighty for his Son, of watching over him, of snatching him from death when he is threatened. He is the one who will introduce Jesus to work, to this abrupt encounter with the concrete, to this realism which permeates everything in Nazareth, even the Aramaic language: "Every Semitic word is tied to two concrete realities: the reality of the mouth which pronounces it and the reality of the object which it designates."[5]

This world is one of visible and invisible reality. Angels are not abstract beings for the Jews; they are, in their own way, as real as the wood used by the carpenter.[6]

What can we say about this family liturgy which is presided over by the father? How intense, without any doubt, is the prayer of these three persons who are increasingly becoming aware of the mystery that unites them!

Why did Jesus leave his parents? The whole significance of this episode is what interests us. He knows that "a man leaves his father and his mother and clings to his wife, and they become one flesh"

(Gn 2:24). He knows he has come to establish a New Covenant: he wants the marriage of humanity with this divine Wisdom, which he incarnates in depth, to take place in him. He is the Wisdom[7] toward which his Father directs the profound aspirations of true hearts: "I loved her and sought her from my youth; I desired to take her for my bride, and became enamoured of her beauty" (Ws 8:2). Jesus is preparing himself for mysterious nuptials, very difficult to describe, for they are the spiritual realities that St. Paul was to interpret in the Letter to the Ephesians as the marriage of Christ and the Church. Authors of spiritual books, especially St. Teresa and St. John of the Cross also described these realities from their own experience. At the heart of his mission, just before he is delivered over to his enemies, during the Last Supper, Jesus will give his body to the Church, like the bridegroom gives himself to the bride.

His parents find him, on the third day, that is, at the biblical moment (there are countless examples of this in the Bible) when great dramas unravel themselves. Mary tells him something he does not seem to understand: "Son, why have you treated us like this? Look, your father and I have been searching for you in great anxiety!" (Lk 2:48).

What is obviously puzzling to him is partly the anguish of this couple so profoundly united to God, as if God himself were distressed; it is also, partly, this expression of Mary's that sounds very strange to Jesus' ears: "Your father is searching for you. . . .!" But his Father is God himself! Mary never lies, she does not make mistakes, she does not make up stories. What does she mean? "Did you not know that I must be in my Father's house?" (Lk 2:49) says Jesus as he opposes his Father to this man of whom Mary is speaking.

What follows speaks for itself: Joseph and Mary do not understand what he is saying and Jesus begins a descent in their footsteps. His feet will obey Mary. Soon, in the humble workshop, his hands will obey Joseph: "Whatever the Father does, the Son does likewise'' (Jn 5:19). Jesus considers Joseph as his father. His feet and hands have designated him!

Jesus had gone up to Jerusalem, to the most beautiful place in the world, to the temple of God; there he had enjoyed immediate respect in spite of his early youth. He descends to a scorned place, Nazareth. And that, through Mary.

3. THE WILL OF THE FATHER

Jesus seeks but one thing: the Father. His first word like his last is directed to the Father from whom he comes and to whom he wants to bring all humans. He is one with the Father in the Spirit: the Father is the very source of his joy and fruitfulness. But it seems that, as man, he has agreed to ignore certain aspects of the will of the Father or, at least, to discover them but one step at a time, as humans do. Some day, he will say this about the mystery of time: ''Neither the angels, nor even the Son . . .'' know the hour of the final event, of the end of history.[8]

Everything happens as if Mary were helping Jesus to choose this carpenter he had just left to be his guide and educator in preference to the learned of the temple. There is, in this scene of St. Luke, a kind of prophetic intervention on Mary's part which precisely recalls the scene of Cana described by St. John. Here, Mary makes Jesus go from the temple to the Holy Family. In Cana, on the contrary, she makes him come out of the Holy Family and gives him the opportunity to perform his first miracle which reveals who he is to everyone there. Oddly enough, John places, immediately after the Cana episode, the other scene of the temple where Jesus chases out the merchants in conditions which are strictly the opposite to what they were in his childhood. This sacred dwelling has become a commercial center of dubious character. His mission is really urgent. In both cases, the will of the Father is expressed through Mary.

This is the most startling and the least known aspect of this will of the Father and of this encounter, of which Mary is the key, between Jesus and the one Mary designates as his father to whom henceforth everything will be subjected. Joseph is the one that "the Father, from whom every family in heaven and on earth takes its name" (Ep 3:15), will vest with his authority.

In order to have some glimpse of this astonishing mystery, one must turn to the inimitable wording used by St. John Eudes: Mary and Jesus are but one heart, something which is true to a unique degree, since Jesus' whole physical being was formed in Mary and since the purity of their love is unequalled. But Mary and Joseph are one heart alone because, for once, two human beings of exceptional purity, courage and inspiration, are united by the bonds of marriage of which the profound significance, since the beginning, is unity in communion. There is here, as it were, a twofold masterpiece of the Holy Spirit, perfectly simple, harmonized, unified: "Once God has spoken; twice have I heard this . . ." (Ps 62:11). We witness two operations when in fact there is only one.

The admirable consequence at the heart of this scene in the temple is the perfect unity of heart of Jesus and Joseph in the heart of Mary. Such is the logical conclusion drawn by St. John Eudes. Such is the secret of the life of the Holy Family. This dialogue, silent to our ears, of Jesus and his father on earth is a total mystery; but how can one not perceive its unfathomable beauty? How can one not sense that here, in Mary, there is a kind of absolutely unprecedented relationship between man and God that justifies the audacities of St. John of the Cross: "And there is no need to wonder that the soul should be capable of aught so high; for, since God grants her the favor of attaining to being deiform and united in the Most Holy Trinity, wherein she becomes God by participation, how is it a thing incredible that she should perform her work of understanding, knowledge and love in the Trinity, together with It, like the Trinity Itself, by a mode of participation, which God effects in the soul itself?''⁹

It pleased God that Joseph should be the first to have experienced these wonders in Mary. As for us, it is in Joseph and Mary that we are called to experience them.

4. A TRUE DESCENT

One cannot help but think that this descent of Jesus, tearing himself away from the temple, was profoundly painful, like Bernadette tearing herself away from Lourdes, her cherished land, her only land, and from the house of her father. Jesus, like Abraham, also leaves his land and the house of his father, to go down into a sort of abjection, of silence and anonymity which stupefied and fascinated Bossuet, Charles de Foucauld and so many others.

Joseph is, as it were, a monitor in the art of death similar to that of the grain of wheat. He gives, without meaning to, a concrete turn to this descent into the incarnation on which St. Paul meditates in one of the most beautiful texts of the Bible, in chapter 2 of the Letter to the Philippians, a text he possibly based on a liturgical hymn.

Jesus leaves the ancient Jerusalem which will keep on drifting toward increasingly dangerous perspectives. By his presence and his unique radiance, he transforms the house of Joseph into the New Jerusalem, the new world hidden behind humble appearances. These two worlds, the Old and the New Jerusalem, gradually move away from each other like two continents.

During Jesus' childhood, the temple and the Holy Family coincide perfectly: Joseph and Mary were at home there. They were amazed at the divine prophecies they heard, they were moved as they took part in the liturgy of praise. The breath of the Spirit of God was blowing in the temple.

When Jesus is twelve, his parents are like intruders in this temple. They no longer understand what is going on there, and in spite of his success, they bring their son away from it.

When Jesus is thirty, he himself no longer recognizes anything in it: he is the one who has become the true temple where the Father is worshipped "in spirit and in truth."

Outside the Holy Family, everything tends to go adrift, to deteriorate; "the evil one," as St. John says, can find himself at home (1 Jn 5:19). In the Holy Family, on the contrary, everything increases in size and in strength "before God and men." Jesus learns the secrets of this descent of the incarnation.

At thirty, Jesus will have the courage and the humility to go down into the waters of the Jordan on the occasion of his baptism in spite of John the Baptist's protests. He joins the sinners to snatch them from death.

Because of them, he will go down to the rank of evildoers, in order to die the most ignominious death invented by men. He, the Living One, will go down into death. He will descend to the bottom of hell.

That is why St. Luke's short verse inaugurating this descent upon Mary's word and in the footsteps of this couple for which Joseph is responsible, is so profoundly moving: "He went down with them" (Lk 2:51). Jesus, then, chooses to go down because this is the will of the Father.

Some day, symbolically, he will live this descent before his apostles, frozen on the spot with shock, at the most solemn moment of his existence, at the moment of the Last Supper, introduced in such a grandiose manner by St. John. "Jesus, knowing that the Father had given all things into his hands, and that he had come from God and was going to God" (Jn 1:3), will fall like a slave at the feet of his apostles to wash their feet, the summit of the Gospel which, for St. John, serves as the account of the institution of the Eucharist. "He humbled himself, and became obedient to the point of death — even death on a cross. Therefore God also highly

exalted him and gave him the name that is above every name . . .''
(Ph 2:8-9).

Mary wants us to know the one who, according to God's plan,
is the secret monitor of this abasement: her husband Joseph.

5. CROSSING A THRESHOLD

When we listen to them, as did Jesus and the saints, Mary and
this silent monitor make us go through stages in the same way that
professors give their students increasingly difficult tasks. And so
St. Teresa of Avila, at the end of her life on the order given by her
superiors, describes the stages of spiritual life in *The Interior
Castle*. She starts from the sordid state of the sinner, lost, burdened,
enslaved to his passions, to attain, in six successive degrees, the
spiritual nuptials, the seventh Mansion, the center and summit of
the human soul.

The great overturn, we have said, occurs midway, at the fourth
Mansion, the starting point of true conversion.

What appears to be indisputable is that, in every life, thresholds
are crossed beyond which things are no longer the same. As we
reflect on this, we shall understand.

First, one must live what Jesus says in the Gospel: ''Unless a
grain of wheat falls into the earth and dies, it remains just a single
grain; but if it dies, it bears much fruit'' (Jn 12:24).

Secondly, one must cross over from a vision where habits in
our ways of thinking and living are too human to a new pulse of life
inspired by the Gospel and very different from the first. This is
what St. Paul expressed forcefully when he says that those ''who
are unspiritual do not receive the gifts of God's Spirit, for they are
foolishness to them, and they are unable to understand them. . . .
Those who are spiritual discern all things, and they are themselves
subject to no one else's scrutiny'' (1 Cor 2:14-15).

Thirdly, in every spiritual journey, there are, as it were, crucial moments when this passage, this death for the sake of life, is relatively clear without always taking on the aspect of a radical break such as we see in the life of St. Paul, when he is thrown down to the ground on the road to Damascus, blinded, directly challenged by Jesus.

What Teresa of Avila calls the fourth Mansion is this central experience which can be lived in thousands of ways. It often is a difficult ordeal; man gives up his limited human logic, his thoughts as man, as Jesus says to Peter, his self-sufficiency as an adult, to open himself to the radically new experience which comes from God, this childlike trust that the genius of Thérèse of the Child Jesus expressed better than anyone else.

Jesus had gone up to the temple; he comes down from it. The temple represents the world of human goodwill which is liable to fall back on itself and bypass life as did the Pharisees.

The Holy Family is the world of communication in which one constantly progresses. It is the world of communion.

In simplified terms, one could say that the temple is this beautiful construction that man can realize in the first phase of his spiritual life with the help of God. It aptly expresses the summit of the first three mansions, of man's new spiritual beginning. In the Holy Family, in a very humble and hidden way, almost indescribable since it is so simple and so new, it is the Lord himself who makes us accede to the gradual discovery of love and liberty in the Spirit.

The fourth Mansion is the descent, disconcerting, very trying at times, but which bears incomparable fruit as one moves from one state into the other. The descent of the head into the heart!

By having recourse to all the languages possible and, especially, to that of the Bible, that of the history of the People of God, we shall attempt to determine these truths more clearly by reminding ourselves of one point: everything here is more a matter of experience than of speech, of a style of life and thought to be discovered rather than to be demonstrated.

It is through the hands and the feet that one becomes the disciple of the one of whom the Pharaoh was already saying through the person of his famous ancestor and image, Joseph, son of Jacob: ''Without your consent no one shall lift up hand or foot in all the land of Egypt'' (Gn 41:44).

ANNEX: *THE FOURTH MANSION*

Certain ways of perceiving the apostolate, certain theological or catechetical discourses of the years following the Council and, most especially, the difficult times inaugurated by the student riots of May 1968, have appeared to me to be characteristic of this world shaped by man's goodwill, of the ''scientific'' analyses which belong to the third Mansion. Like many, possibly more than others at times, I have suffered from this. This text, published in *La Croix*, September 28, 1978, when I was a professor in a private secondary school in the South-West of France, represents a painful practical exercise that I have attempted to express in this chapter. I had been confronted for some time with those kinds of discourses, frequent at this time, where it seemed to me that the essential was missing. A kind of irrepressible uneasiness had, as it were, drawn this cry from me:

''In short, we often find ourselves at the summit of the third Mansion of St. Teresa of Avila's *Interior Castle*. At the summit of what St. Paul calls the 'unspiritual man,' in chapter 2 of the First Letter to the Corinthians, of the very well-organized, courageous, lucid, brotherly human nature, but then, as Jesus says, 'pagans do as much' (something which is excellent as everyone agrees).

''As soon as we reach the fourth Mansion, the beautiful convictions, the best sociological analyses emanating from the best diocesan centers, all the more so, the 'scientific' idle dreams of Marxism, all of that become strangely relative. Why? Very simply because the folly of God has begun to filter into the wisdom of humans. A little breath of the Holy Spirit has passed by, something as whimsical as the wind. I recall Father de la Pommeraie speaking to us in the seminary in Rome, twenty-five years ago, on the mystical 'nights' experienced by militant laborers. Fredo Krumnow, whom I met in unforgettable circumstances, also gave this impression.

"The fourth Mansion is about the hesitant beginnings of spiritual life. The prominently active people in the Church, those who have stirred masses and, even without seeking to do so, have forced the evolution of these famous social structures that had to be changed, they are these men and women, such as St. Bernard or Mother Teresa, who have learned to take a stand, face down to the ground.

"I know, it is terrible to write such things, for if the one who writes them is not serious about them himself, he will be severely reprimanded by the Lord for his useless words. But even if I am very small in the social ladder, I suffer terribly, like many, from our exploits in the third Mansion. How many have given up, how many 'recycled' priests and religious women are, in fact, condemned to despair or to arrogance because they were launched in undefined paths, condemned to 'espouse the human' in every sense of the word? What a mess? And let us not say that this is of Christ's making. He has chosen for himself in this world this bride which is the Church, which he is painfully trying to adorn and purify. St. John says so; she is no more of this world.

"What a ray of hope it is to see so many men and women, so many young people who try to open themselves to the Spirit in truth! When we think of the relationship existing between the Father and the Son, in the Spirit, we are thinking of that very relationship that Jesus wants to establish with us: 'As the Father has loved me, so I have loved you' (Jn 15:9). Precisely, the same relationship.''

1 The great philosopher Maurice Blondel constantly meditated on this mystery of the growth of Christ, the growth of his conscience which supposes obscurities, efforts, discoveries. It is there that Christ reaches us and we reach him. "The growth of Christ, the fundamental theme of the infancy narratives in Luke, is not, in this existence, a superficial or marginal adventure; it is at the very heart of the way Jesus lives his experience of being Son of God." Guillet, *Jésus devant sa vie et sa mort*, Aubier, 1971, p. 57.

2 *The Complete Works of St. Teresa of Jesus*, op. cit., vol. 2, *Interior Castle*, p. 230.

3 St. Maximus the Confessor died a martyr in 662 to defend the truth of the existence of both a human will and a divine will in Christ, fully divine and fully human.

4 Much has been written about this scene in St. Luke: R. Laurentin, *Jésus au temple*, Gabalda, 1966; *Les Évangiles de l'Enfance*, DDB, 1982; Robert Aron, *Jesus of Nazareth: the hidden years*. Trans. Frances Frenaye, Hamish Hamilton, London, 1962.

5 Aron, *op. cit.*, p. 33.

6 R. Laurentin, *Les Évangiles de l'Enfance*, p. 468.

7 On this theme, see the study by A. Feuillet, *Le Christ, Sagesse de Dieu*, Gabalda, 1966.

8 "This statement revealing his ignorance very soon shocked his listeners. It is tactfully glossed over in the parallel text of Luke 21:33. We gratefully set it down today as a precious testimony to the humanity of Jesus." J. Guillet, *Jésus devant sa vie et sa mort*, Aubier, 1971, p. 194.

9 *The Complete Works of St. John of the Cross*, translated and edited by E. Allison Peers, 3rd revised ed., 3 vols. Newman Press, 1953, *Spiritual Canticle*, 38, vol. 2, p. 168.

CHAPTER V

The Father's Shadow

1. THE PATERNAL TRIAL

AT the age of twelve, Jesus made a descent of which we sense the immense impact. All his profound training, all the rest of his life and, consequently, our salvation, our hope, and our lives, intimately linked with his, are interested in this trip Jesus made from Jerusalem to Nazareth.

It recalls another trip which dominates the whole Bible and therefore the whole history of humanity: the Exodus, the journey the Jewish people had to make from the land of Egypt to the Promised Land.

In fact, at the outset, these unfortunate Jews, who had been the slaves of the powerful Egyptians for more than four centuries, were not even a nation. They were a motely collection of poor, burdened, crushed people, in the midst of whom some fugitives were hiding: little by little, thanks to Moses, their leader, and especially thanks to divine protection, thanks to the Law and to the whole new organization that it would bring about, this human flock would organize itself, humanize itself, become the People of God.

The ordeal of the desert, so long and so harsh, the long purification, as terrible as it was admirable, would complete their education and leave them with the greatest memories. The prophets and the psalms constantly refer to them. God seems to recall these times of blessings with emotion in spite of their harshness: "When Israel was a child, I loved him . . . I . . . taught Ephraim to walk, I took them up in my arms . . . I was to them like those who lift infants to their cheeks" (Ho 11:1-4).

Why? Because this time spent in the desert, these forty years which separate the period of penal servitude from the settlement in the land of all promises, is essentially, as it were, a revelation of the fatherly love of God:

"Remember the long way that the Lord your God has led you these forty years in the wilderness, in order to humble you, testing you to know what was in your heart, whether or not you would keep his commandments. . . . Know then in your heart that as a parent disciplines a child so the Lord your God disciplines you" (Dt 8:2, 5).

Behind this apparent severity there was an immense love.

"I took them up in my arms; but they did not know that I healed them! I led them with cords of human kindness, with bands of love. . . ." (Ho 11:3-4).

"I thought how I would set you among my children, and give you a pleasant land, the most beautiful heritage of all the nations. And I thought you would call me, My Father, and would not turn from following me. . . ." (Jr 3:19).

All the mysteries of Christian life and, consequently, of human life, viewed in all their dimensions — for God is the Creator, the Master of history, the Savior — are symbolically of the departure, the night of the Passover when the Jews celebrate their liberation around the lamb, during a meal where the blood of this lamb protects them; whether it be the crossing of the Red Sea, the image of baptism, of the manna, the image of the Eucharist; whether it be the gift of the Law, the divine presence in the Ark of the Covenant and the countless ordeals experienced, everything speaks to us of the Christian mystery.

The significance of these forty years is clear: to draw men away from an idolatrous world where everyone is a slave, from the miserable man groaning under the foreman's lashes to the Pharaoh enslaved to his vices and superstitions. To set men on their course toward the discovery of the true face of God, through the experience of this Jewish people, born of Abraham, Isaac and Jacob, patriarchs chosen by the Most High. Should one wish to sum up this whole journey in one sentence, a journey as trying as it was essential, one could say: God wanted to make humanity cross a threshold by revealing himself as Father and not as a tyrant.

According to the very logic of what we were discovering in our fourth stage — for the "style of God," as St. John of the Cross says, is fundamentally strictly true to itself — these forty years are, as it were, the historical version, as grandiose as it can be in spite of its modest appearances, comparable to the fantastic frescoes of human existence in Teresa of Avila's fourth Mansion.

The number forty will become the symbol of a passage, denoting a profound transformation, whether it be these forty years in the desert, or the forty days Moses spent on Mount Sinai, or Elijah's march of forty days to Mount Horeb, or the forty days that separate the first phase of Jesus' life, when he is incomparably protected in the world of Nazareth, from the second phase when he will challenge Satan every day.

Our entire life is a journey through the desert. If, through the Spirit of Jesus, we recognize there the holy forty days, as Lent invites us to do, everything changes. We are no longer whimpering slaves always tempted to go back to the slavery of Egypt: we gradually become sons (cf Dt 8:5).

An essential reality will help us to do that: the cloud.

2. THE CLOUD

No biblical reality is more important than the pillar of cloud for the poor humans that we are, for it sums up all of God's operations.

It is, so to speak, the perfect image of the work of the Spirit. Whenever they recalled the pillar of cloud that accompanied the Hebrews in their peregrinations, the Jews of the Middle Ages thought of a kind of maternal power, the protector of the community.

This pillar of cloud has no other alternative but death. Indeed, if God does not show himself, man is no more than an unfortunate individual gone astray, marked by death, like Adam chased from paradise. If God shows himself, this also means death for he says: "No one shall see me and live" (Ex 33:20). Hidden in the cleft of a rock, Moses was able to see God "from the back" — like Bernadette who had glimpses of unknown glimmers and beauties. The cloud reveals by concealing. The Book of Exodus, with its forty chapters (like the forty years in the desert it begins to relate) is entirely devoted to the glory of this cloud. It is through it that the Lord makes his people cross over from the state of slavery to that of freedom in "a land flowing with milk and honey" (Jos 5:7). The pillar of cloud has led the whole operation, blinding the evil ones who, unknowingly, are manipulated by the Devil, so powerful in the world (cf 1 Jn 5:19); enlightening the poor, the beloved of God, in the night of their Exodus.

This cloud displays an untiring solitude, leading the column to point out the road or staying in the rear to lead the enemy astray allowing an irreversible crossing of the Red Sea. "God thought, 'If the people face war, they may change their minds and return to Egypt' " (Ex 13:17). Something that would have irremediably compromised everything! This cloud manifests the secret of the Father's love, a merciful love, a maternal love, as Hosea, Isaiah and other prophets understood so well: "The Most High . . . will love you more than does your mother. . . ." (Si 4:10). At the same time, this cloud commands as an exacting and demanding Father would do. It must be obeyed both night and day. As he sums up his thought, the author of Exodus concludes his work by contemplating this wonder one last time: "Whenever the cloud was taken up from the tabernacle, the Israelites would set out on each stage of their journey; but if the cloud was not taken up, then they did not set out until the day that it was taken up. For the cloud of the Lord was on the tabernacle by day, and fire was in the cloud by night, before the eyes of all the house of Israel at each stage of their journey'' (Ex 40:36-38).

Indeed, as the Jewish thinkers had felt, this cloud has a maternal side to it although it expresses the mystery of the Father. It perfectly represents the Father acting through his Spirit to raise sons in the Son. It expresses exactly what the couple Joseph and Mary will become, Joseph providing shelter for Mary at the service of the incarnation, the shadow of the holy marriage.

But, how is it introduced in the Book of Exodus?

By a mysterious reality, almost magic, so powerful, hidden and disconcerting it is (this magic obviously has nothing to do with men's imitations of it with the help of the father of lies); it deals with the bones of Joseph, son of Jacob. At the time of his death, the fourth patriarch, the savior of the people of God, had made his descendants take a solemn oath. They had to promise they would bring back his remains into the land of Jacob, his father, the land of the Promise. The destiny of that man is one of the most remarkable one can find, it is absolutely unique in the Bible. He was his father's favorite son for several reasons, some of which were his handsome appearance and his intelligence as well as the circumstances of his conception (Jacob loved Rachel, his mother). Envied and hated by his brothers, sold as a slave, he became the all-powerful prime minister of the mightiest country of the world at the time. He had, as one could say, inaugurated the Gospel forgiveness before the letter, and left the memory of a man inhabited by the Spirit of God. Married to the daughter of a priest of the Egyptian aristocracy, his role was unlimited, new and vast as it was.[1] At the time of his death, this patriarch expressed himself as follows: " 'I am about to die; but God will surely come to you, and bring you up out of this land to the land that he swore to Abraham, to Isaac, and to Jacob.' So Joseph made the Israelites swear, saying, 'When God comes to you, you shall carry up my bones from here.' And Joseph died, being one hundred and ten years old; he was embalmed and placed in a coffin in Egypt'' (Gn 50:24-26).

When one reflects on what embalming meant to the great ones of Egypt, and on the mystery of the pyramids, one can imagine the significance of the relics of a man so prodigiously inspired. We can see that; God's visitation and his powerful action with a strong hand and a vigorous arm is linked, according to this express prophecy, with the transfer of his bones. The bones of Joseph are what directly introduce the immeasurable blessings of the divine cloud, as the author of Exodus clearly says (cf Ex 13:19).[2]

The importance of this cloud, ''dark on one side and luminous on the other'' (cf Ex 14:20), is not confined to life in the desert. We constantly find it whenever God is approaching. When Yahweh wishes to speak to Moses, at the high moments of the covenant; when the priests want to celebrate the consecration of the new temple at the time of Solomon, the cloud is there, splendid and awesome. Ezekiel and all of Judaism recall its presence with emotion for it will be the sign of the return of God: ''The glory of the Lord and the cloud will appear, as they were shown in the case of Moses, and as Solomon asked that the temple be gloriously consecrated'' (2 M 2:8).

3. THE SHADOW OF THE ALMIGHTY

When we speak of the cloud, we are not talking about a mythical invention we could attribute to the imagination of the writers of the biblical text but about a reality, a reality of which we live today, unaware of it most of the time. Starting from Jesus, the preparations, promises, images of the Old Testament become reality, a total spiritual realization. We can say along with Philip: ''We have found him about whom Moses in the law and also the prophets wrote, Jesus son of Joseph from Nazareth'' (Jn 1:45). As we have already said, and this is important, there is nothing abstract in the Bible. This cloud, which acts like the loving and vigilant presence of the Father trying, through the Holy Spirit, to make his unfortunate children evolve from the status of slaves to that of heir princes, must have a yet more concrete face in the New Covenant. This cloud is there spiritually, accompanying the least initiatives of the heart of a believer. It is not an abstraction. It represents the concrete conditioning which, as a whole, makes the reflexes of a man guided by faith in Jesus Christ in the realm of thought and action different from those of the unbeliever.

What we have slowly discovered is beginning to fall into place. The ancient Joseph is thus the prophet of this cloud, and his bones are what introduce him directly (in the same way that Bernadette's tombstone in the chapel of St. Joseph is a witness to a unique story). Our Joseph, as St. Francis de Sales would say, is the one who conceals the incarnation and guides it: he alone receives the light of the angels from the Almighty for this role. It is uniquely because of this man of the night that the intelligence of the learned of Israel is confused, that the police of the cruel potentate Herod are tricked, that the Devil, so subtle when it comes to do harm, seems to be ignorant of his prey. At one with his wife, he embodies this loving shadow to perfection, a shadow possessing an invincible power in its apparent weakness and unequalled tenderness.

Together, they are the two conditions for the work of the Holy Spirit who is pursuing but one goal: to be able at least ''to groan'' in the heart of humanity with the ''unutterable groanings'' of the Son lovingly saying to his Father: Abba, Daddy, this Father who is acknowledged at last.

When commenting on the Latin translation of the Greek text of the Nicene Creed (381), St. Augustine gives an awesome touch to the words *Pater omnipotens*. Instead of being the one ''who makes everything hold together'' (*pantocrator*), by supporting ''from

under,'' like a father holding his small child because it is everything to him, the Father becomes a kind of Caesar from above, who
makes mighty decisions, who predestines human beings to this and
to that.[3] After the terrible crisis which almost overcame him in
Paris, St. Francis de Sales, the young student in Padua, again
experienced real torture for having attempted to pose these insolu-
ble questions. Fortunately, in Jesus Christ, who came between
Joseph and Mary, he ended up by emerging within the Holy Family
of Nazareth and was thus able to see things from a totally different
perspective as he explains in his masterly book *Treatise on the Love
of God.*

God imposed two conditions for the coming of his Son and,
consequently, for the absolutely unique gift linked with this coming, the gift of the Holy Spirit: Joseph and Mary, two human
beings, perfectly humble, simple, brave, defenceless and,
nevertheless, endowed with a strength and a kind of superiority so
indisputable that ''the image of the invisible God, the firstborn of
all creation'' (Col 1:15), chose to be subjected to them.

Mary is the one in whom the Holy Spirit makes the Body of
Christ come, a fact which, with time, assumes the proportions of
the Church in the midst of humanity; Joseph is the one in whom the
Father conceals himself to welcome this child and, in turn, to hide
it, to surround it with love, to protect it, to help it increase in every
way. ''The Holy Spirit will come upon you,'' the angel said to
Mary, ''and the power of the Most High will overshadow you'' (Lk
1:35). Joseph is the Father's shadow. He is directly foreshadowed
by this biblical cloud, an exact prolongation of the fourth patriarch.

As in the case of the cloud, it is striking to see that these mortal
enemies, whom St. Paul calls ''cosmic powers,'' our true enemies,
he says (cf Ep 6:12), can do absolutely nothing against this fragile
Infant, so avidly spied upon by misunderstanding and hostility.

At twelve, upon one word spoken by his mother, a word he
does not immediately understand, Jesus must identify ''to be
with his Father'' — his most cherished wish — with ''to be with

Joseph." And he disappears in this "shadow" where, surprisingly, he will grow in stature and in strength for a period of eighteen years. I cannot help but think that such a mystery, this long and profound formation, would have lasting effects on the entire life of Jesus as well as on the life of the Church of all ages.

Mary seems to disappear, after the Cana episode, until we find her again at the foot of the Cross, at the most solemn of moments. There, according to St. John, Jesus is fulfilling the Scriptures (cf Jn 19:28) to perfection by giving her up to be the Mother of humanity represented by St. John himself. She embodies the "heart of mercy" mentioned in Zechariah's hymn, after the prophet Isaiah, the ultimate secret of God.

Is Joseph, on the one hand, totally absent from his inseparable wife in this supreme ordeal and, on the other, from the one who had become his much beloved son, his close companion for so long? We have said so above; Joseph must disappear completely from the scene when Jesus begins his mission, for there must not be the slightest ambiguity when Jesus is speaking about his Father. Joseph disappears. He knows perfectly well how to do this: this is his specialty, to hide his person and the persons of those entrusted to him. However, one would have a poor knowledge of the Father, the source of all fatherhood, of all generosity, if one thought, as our Protestant brothers believe, that Christ used Mary and Joseph and then forgot all about them. It was in Joseph, for all eternity, that Jesus had learned to say "Father!" This basic experience of the heart of Jesus introduced absolutely mysterious bonds between the eternal Father and the humble Joseph, bonds which are precisely this mystery into which we are called upon to enter.

How can one not think that he was at the heart of this dramatic scene when, fulfilling the Scriptures to the end by obeying the will of the Father and accepting the obligations of this human condition slowly learnt in Nazareth, Jesus would cry out this name for the last time, with a love that would forever unsettle the empire of death:

"Father, into your hands I commend my spirit . . ." (Lk 23:46). The cloud then took the form of a sort of darkness that hid the sun for three hours as if the Father wished to veil his Son from an unbelieving world as if he wanted to accompany him in his suffering, discreetly, lovingly, in the same style he had precisely used for thirty years through the cherished presence of Joseph.

As for the new tomb, this hollowed-out rock which had never been used and which would be the witness to his resurrection, the triumph of the Spirit of the Father, it belonged to a certain Joseph in the same way that the virgin womb of Mary where this same Holy Spirit had operated the incarnation had been entrusted to Joseph. This did not happen by chance. Joseph is an important name in the Bible: it determined not only a person but also a role. Joseph, either in person or by mysterious spiritual presence which can only be hinted at, is in charge of keeping watch over the Body of Christ.

What interpretation should be given to all these rapprochements? It is impossible to say. Joseph's experience of fatherhood alone, the kind Jesus had known for so long under his direction, can offer some element of an answer. The Church has quite mysteriously acknowledged him to be the patron saint of a happy death, not only because his death was incomparably assisted by the presence of Jesus and Mary, as is supposed, but also because he seems to have been predestined to prepare humans to die. Is not Jesus the first one who might have benefited from this?

Should not this obscure cloud which surrounds the coming of Jesus and his slow training and education with Joseph be compared to the one which surrounds his death and resurrection? Does it not have some obscure ties with this luminous cloud which, having hidden the Ascension, will accompany the coming of the Son of Man in glory?

4. A UNIQUE PROPHECY

We are baffled, we are moving ahead one step at a time in this new unknown world; we experience the need to be guided, comforted.

We shall have an unexpected support in a special prophecy we find in St. Ignatius of Antioch, a bishop of the first century, who died a martyr in Rome in about the year 107, one of the most inspired Christian thinkers there is. In his letter to the Ephesians, he writes: "The maidenhood of Mary and her child-bearing and also the death of the Lord were hidden from the prince of this world — three resounding mysteries wrought in the silence of God" (XIX, 1).

No one can deny that men, even the learned ones of Israel, have ignored the virgin conception of Jesus because of the presence of Joseph. St. Ignatius goes further: he claims that this superior spirit, Satan himself, was unaware of it, as if Joseph were a screen, opaque to the spirits themselves, these spirits who, according to St. Paul, are the true enemies of humanity (Ep 6:12). As the Egyptians let their slaves flee and were unable to catch up with them because of the cloud which protected them, so Joseph confused all those who could not accept the incarnation.

As far as the third point is concerned, the relationship between Joseph and the biblical cloud allows us to sense how Joseph spiritually helped Jesus to escape the Devil in the acts of his death on the cross, when death is overcome by life, a truth the resurrection will conveys for all times.

Instead of calling to his help more than twelve legions of angels, whom his Father would have sent him immediately (cf Mt 26:53), Jesus will live what he has learned for a long time with Joseph: respect for the Scriptures and the total acceptance of his human condition such as he experienced it in Nazareth. He will hand over to the executioner his hands and feet which have been under Joseph's orders for so long as he performed his humble tasks in the name of the Father. The terribly miserable nature of the death of this man, who was condemned, booed by the crowd, scorned by the great, condemned to the death of a slave, will utterly mislead the Devil. Thinking he was victorious, he is definitely defeated. The shadow of the Father, evoked by the darkness accompanying this death, played its role to the end, up to the last cry to the Father; like an explosion of silence, Joseph helped Jesus to die like a man.

But St. Ignatius goes on: "A star shone in the heavens, brighter than all the other stars, and its light was indescribable, and its newness astonished, and all the other stars, along with the sun and the moon, took their places as a choir surrounding the star, and it projected its light more than all the others. And they were disturbed, wondering where this newness so different from themselves came from. Then all magic was destroyed, and all sites of evil abolished, ignorance was dispelled and the old kingdom ruined, as God appeared in the shape of a man to bring about a newness of eternal life [cf. Rm 6:4]. What had been decided by God was beginning to be realized. Hence, everything was perturbed, for the destruction of death was being prepared" (XIX, 2).

It is through this star that the three mysteries mentioned, the conception of Jesus, his birth and the death of the Lord, must be manifested to the centuries.

The theme of this legend is clear: it recalls the star that led the Magi to the Child and Mary his mother (cf Mt 2:11). It also recalls the dream of the ancient Joseph, a direct image of the new one, before whom the sun, the moon and eleven stars bowed down (cf Gn 37:9).

From that moment all is clear. The one who is given the duty by the Most High of concealing the newness of what is being prepared in silence and in the night is also the one who will introduce all humans to the treasure entrusted to him, the child and his mother, a unique treasure. Joseph is like this star whose newness is so radical, so baffling that no one sees or understands it, except the few witnesses we met who are visited by an exceptional grace from God. Some day this star will no longer go unnoticed, to the amazement of masters and thinkers, of authorities of all kinds, of Magi of every origin, magnetically drawn by the perfection of the wisdom that they will see in its domains.

Meanwhile, let us consider the day when Brother André left this earth in Montreal, he who, along with the humble Bernadette, can be thought of as St. Joseph's most outstanding prophet. He died on January 6, 1937, on the feast of the Epiphany when the Church meditates on the mysterious star which leads all the wise of the world to the divine Wisdom in the form of a tiny child.

As for human magic with all its spells and its claims, all its obscurantist and evil groping, so powerful today among the sects, it will vanish like smoke before the splendor of the true. Then will come the full revelation of Joseph's world of which Jesus and Mary were both the first architects and the first beneficiaries. Joseph works only for this unknown, amazing, indescribable world of beauty which is that of the child and Mary his mother.

5. THE SHADOW'S FIRST BLESSING

This divine shadow possesses an astonishing power, as the Egyptians found out to their own amazement (cf Nb 14:9), but it does not behave in the manner of the "protective shadows" of the other peoples (cf Nb 14:9), the divinities which shield against the formidable heat of the sun, which render services, which confer powers but make no demands. The divine shadow is a living one and is demanding. It does not exempt from effort, trials, necessary privations, paternal discipline which is often harsh. It has the exigencies of a love which is true, humble, perfectly gentle at times but perfectly rigorous at others. This shadow confers none of the automatic superiorities one seeks in magic, in superstitions, in the ordinary "religious" bereft of faith. Who has been more tried than

Joseph himself? The trials of the first make us foresee those of the second, the great Joseph. The Egyptians themselves acknowledged the boundless gift from the God who inhabits them (and this gift is none other than the Spirit of God): "Can we find anyone else like this — one in whom is the spirit of God?" (Gn 41:38). They paid most dearly for this gift. This is what Teresa of Avila, at the end of the sixth Mansion, whispers in the ear of those who are foolish enough to desire certain gifts which appear enviable to them, as they did to Simon the magician: "Do you suppose that the trials suffered by those to whom the Lord grants these favors are light ones? No, they are very heavy, and of many kinds. How do you know if you would be able to bear them?"[4]

Strictly speaking, the stakes are much higher than we, poor creatures of flesh and blood, can imagine. Our true enemies are not humans, says St. Paul, but spirits, as inept as they are desperate, formless. They belong neither to the earth (where God protects us with his "cloud," Joseph, when we are not too unreasonable), nor to heaven from which they were banished by Michael (cf Rv 12:9). They want to harm us in the only space they have left, the "in-between space," which belongs to the evil one as Jesus warns us (cf Mt 5:37). That is why Paul calls them "the powers of the air, the powers of the middle way" (cf Ep 2:2), the powers of ambiguity, of equivocation, of confusion. Such powers, along with the stupid complicity of humans, are what pervert the language. In the same way that the created being begins with "the Word," as St. John says, so illusion and deceit, which are the precise negation of the Word, begin with the perversion of language. This is what is shown in the episode of the tower of Babel: the dream of humans, cut off from God, is to establish one single tower, a task common to all and which serves as a rallying point for men, one sole language, one sole compulsory ideology by which the strong necessarily dominate the weak, with the feeble and slothful complicity of the latter.

People think they are speaking one sole language and they no longer understand each other: people think they are unifying society in a common task and they all hate each other; people think they are creating liberty and all are slaves, from the smallest to the greatest. These false solutions can perpetuate themselves in a horrible way, making humans lose the very notion of liberty and, consequently, the wish to come out of such a situation. The only thing God can do is to disperse this ant hill.

Examples of this cruel perversion of language can be gathered like dead leaves or, more precisely, like dirty litter left behind by ill-bred crowds. Kindness is confused with stupidity. Human stupidity is, basically, the first and the greatest support of the evil one in his work of perversion. Without stupidity, evil would eventually decrease for it goes directly against what we are all seeking.[5]

People confuse rigor and inflexibility. The rigorous discipline of the skater supposes an infinite flexibility: the inflexibility of the moralist is a dangerous caricature. The first thing that Mary silently teaches little Bernadette on February 11, 1858 is precisely to go from this inflexibility in which she had been brought up into the flexible rigor of Joseph's world, Mary's own world. Bernadette must learn, not without being profoundly moved, to make a delightful sign of the cross.

We confuse the necessary autonomy, without which we cannot give ourselves (if you are not autonomous, you are caught, dispossessed, enslaved), with the stupid egotism which ignores the fruitfulness of the gift. We confuse liberty, which is a painful and amazing ascent, with the liberties of unconstraint where we rush down without any hope.

The Devil makes us confused. The Spirit hidden in the cloud, like Mary hidden in Joseph, can help us to make distinctions and with what shrewdness! It is the Spirit of the Son, like a "two-edged sword."

The supreme imposture, the most hidden and the most pernicious, is the one which leans on the powers, so noble, of the sexual instinct. Sexuality, viewed with suspicion in the Western Church especially since St. Augustine, in contrast with the Eastern Church, is one of the most fundamental languages of human life and love. Besides, God has tied it with procreation, a reality which implies a direct collaboration with the act of creating, still more fundamental than work or artistic creation.

Father Fessard has devoted a remarkable study[6] to this topic in which he shows that the sexed condition is not only the basis of true human relationships but the introduction to the understanding of the encounter between God and humans. Humanity is, in face of God, as woman is in face of man. This is why St. Paul says that "woman is the reflection [glory] of man" (1 Cor 11:7). If man discovers the truth about God, as opposed to the idolater, he will rediscover the secret of service, of a profound respect for women, of true love which gives its life for the one loved. Everything becomes possible. Otherwise, relationships become unhappy relationships of strength or perversion.

In an admirable tableau of the mid-fifteenth century, the Crowning of Mary, Enguerrand Charton portrays the Father and the Son as two young men, bearded, of extreme dignity, difficult to identify so much so they resemble each other, both crowning the Virgin Mary in a splendor which pales the most beautiful poetic imaginations. Not the slightest trace of passion, of necessity, here. Everything is characterized by the simplest of liberties. On the contrary, perversion at best mingles a secretly frenzied drive, a secret exploitation, a certain narcissism or the snares of sadomasochism.[7] Even but a trace of it becomes the means through which Satan perverts everything radically, casting suspicion on true tenderness and unleashing a world of violence and madness.

People can say what they like and some will defend themselves, to be sure, before such an apparently blunt and intolerant judgment. Nothing could better point out the difference of appreciation which exists between those to whom the Lord has given the grace to enter into the cloud, into Joseph's workshop, and those who are still only the notables of Israel. The first clearly see why St. Paul spoke with so much clarity on the subject which holds our attention in the first chapters of the Letter to the Romans; the others do not manage to see and they accuse the first. The first discover, not without an exacting vigilance, a joy, a tenderness, a strength, a quality of communion which makes them have a glimpse of what the dialogue between Joseph and Jesus might have been. The others act like everybody else, think like everybody else. The world recognizes them as its own and they just manage to "keep going," as the poet Jules Laforgue used to say.

The examples of these confusions which are so detrimental abound in daily life. Reserve is a liberty, for it keeps us on the threshold of what could embarrass others. It has nothing to do with timidity, this sad bondage, born from old inner chains, which spoils relationships. One must choose between shining, by showing off his little genius and knowledge, and enlightening. Since truth is bound to humility, the one who shines does not enlighten.

Similarly, an intellectualism which handles abstractions with ease is often the enemy of the intelligence which is made for reality. Aggressiveness, indispensable in dealing with difficulties, in defending what we love, must not be confused with unjust violence: the first is useful to fight against the second. There is a humility which abases, the false one; another which elevates, the true one.

Such is the incomparable blessing of Joseph's fatherhood, of the protection of this cloud, of this shadow where Jesus was guided and educated for so long: the Spirit can make us pronounce, along with Joseph, a true "no" to this world of confusion and, without knowing how, we become able to detect clearly what our ignorance, our self-conceit, our panic would have almost fatally led us to confuse.

This advantage, so appreciable, is an introduction to the second blessing of this shadow: to be able to say "yes" with Mary to what the old habits of our reason, the poor routine and obdurate wisdom of the human species (whose mind is still dimmed by various spirits of darkness) could not but oppose.

6. THE SHADOW'S SECOND BLESSING

In an unexpected way, this shadow of the Father brings about in us the death of a whole generation of thoughts and feelings too strongly influenced by Egypt, that is, by the ancient conditioning of the human world, this world which is deluded, enslaved, oblivious to its own slavery, like those Hebrews, impervious to the calls of God and whose bodies strewed the wilderness (Nb 14:29). This operation is far from being easy to perform within us. It goes on constantly if we are somewhat intelligent and faithful at the time of the trials, crises, illnesses, failures, discoveries, joys and wonders we experience. It goes on and we have a clearer view of ourselves, as if the angels, who are the great laborers in Joseph's workshop, were beginning to bind the darnel in order to burn it and garner the eternal harvest.

Then a wonder begins to take shape, a wonder which is the object of the ultimate meditation of the Old Testament: the typical wonder of the Exodus, the real fruit of the fatherly shadow which is the marriage of contradictories, that is of these realities that we cannot but irreducibly oppose. That is found in chapter 19 of the Book of Wisdom, the final chapter of the last book of the Old Covenant written in Alexandria:

> For land animals were transformed into water creatures,
> and creatures that swim moved over to the land.
> Fire even in water retained its normal power,
> and water forgot its fire-quenching nature.
> Flames, on the contrary, failed to consume
> the flesh of perishable creatures
> that walked among them . . . (Ws 19:19-21).

We recognize the world foretold in chapter 11 of Isaiah, where "the wolf shall live with the lamb . . . the nursing child shall play over the hole of the asp, and the weaned child shall put its hand on the adder's den" (Is 11:6, 8).

But here divine action is presented in a yet more striking way: on the one hand, it is linked with the journey in the desert and with the guidance so typical of the divine cloud; on the other, the symbolism used is significant. Many different cultures ended up by resorting to it.

If we wanted to bring things back to the essential, we would say that the basic elements, the earth and the water that makes it fruitful, represent, as it were, the deep fabric of human life, the one that every human being receives from woman, that is, the body, its instincts and the feelings that move us.

Fire and air, on the contrary, the solar world above, dry, precise, evokes rationality, the area of principles, of structures in which male logic feels at ease.

Water is, as it were, the symbol of the first aspect of woman, that of the sensitivity which translates itself through emotions, where the whole being moves like the waves (tears!). It is the world of intuition, of impulse, the precious basis of this kind of élan without which there would be no human life. Fire is the contrasting symbol of the dry and precise reason, efficient and powerful, as well, in a totally different way.

The Spirit alone can allow fire and water to meet, to unite: one could see a proper symbol of this union in blood, liquid like water and red like fire. Blood binds the human body into a unit and a being with the generations preceding and following it. Its importance is vital. That is why the Jews saw in it, as it were, the materialization of the divine breath by which God gave life to the first man. For them, blood is sacred; it must neither be spilled nor eaten.

One can say that the union of water and fire, of sensitivity and reason, the feminine and masculine faces of humanity, express what the Spirit of God alone can do, this union being as indispensable as it is impossible.

The Holy Spirit loves to unite contradictories, but he can do so only in favorable conditions, only in the Holy Family. Why? Because this is the only spiritual space on earth where evil has no access.

What does "contradictories" mean generally? Irreducible affirmations like the true and the false, reality and illusion, deceit and truth, virtue and vice, the world of Christ which is truth and that of Satan, "the father of lies." As soon as one has crossed the threshold of Nazareth, the word takes on another meaning. It designates, for example, the theme on which Dante meditates in the final prayer of his great poem.

> O Virgin Mother, daughter of thy Son,
> Lowly and uplifted more than any creature,
> Fixed goal of the eternal counsel . . . [8]

Everything is astonishing here because the earth, at least, has reached heaven, because the Son of God, "the firstborn of all creation; for in him all things in heaven and on earth were created" (Col 1:15-16), makes himself the tiniest being while the carpenter of Nazareth becomes greater than the greatest of men (cf Mt 11:11), according to Jesus' very words. [9]

This new world is the one Cardinal Nicholas of Cusa, a superior mind as much for his culture as for his intuition, had foreseen in the middle of the fifteenth century: "The place where we will find you unveiled, O my God, I have found it surrounded by the coincidence of contradictories; it is the wall of the paradise you inhabit and to which we will have access only when we have overcome reason which guards its door." [10]

It would be more appropriate to say that reason must accept, through the mysterious movement of the love which carries it along, to renounce its tyrannical pretensions and open itself to what it does not see but is urged to believe.

This is exactly the result to which Joseph and Mary wish to lead us when they beckon us to follow them, as they beckoned Jesus. What might have appeared impossible, or constraining, unpleasant, irrational, becomes relatively simple and the source of surprising discoveries.

One begins to have an idea of the divine interplay of the coincidence of the contradictories like this wonder that all the wise have tried to encompass, especially in the East and the Far East:

> All things come in pairs, one opposite the other,
> and he has made nothing incomplete.
> Each supplements the virtue of the other.
> Who could ever tire of seeing his glory? (Si 42:24-25).

Let us think about this and we shall see that the summit and the source of this wonder is the incarnation to which the key is the couple, Joseph and Mary. They define a space with astonishing properties, the divine space on earth entrusted to the "righteous" Joseph by the Lord.

How could one not be overwhelmed with gratitude at the thought that the blood of Christ (this blood in which all the contradictories are resolved), allows us, poor sinners, to enter into this movement on the strength of our baptism? Certainly, one must accept Joseph's fatherhood, which we shall try to present in the last stage of this book; one must obey this cloud even if one does not always understand. How could we understand a combination as incongruous as strength and weakness, joy and tribulation, life and death, glory and abasement? We can live without understanding and, by living, we can gradually accede to a new understanding. It is the very journey of the Hebrews with respect to the demands of the Law: "All that the Lord has spoken we will do, and we will be obedient'' (Ex 24:7), or, ''we will heed and do.''[11] Here, to heed means to understand, as we have already pointed out. Normally, one understands and then does; in the case of Joseph, one does and then understands.

If we sufficiently and secretly agree with all that St. Thomas terms as ''the instinct of the Holy Spirit,'' rather than only with our short-sighted reason, we enter then into the logic of the saints, a logic which is often disconcerting. Mother Agnès shows this in a letter written on July 16, 1897 to the Guérins, her family, about her sister Thérèse whose health is in a very poor state: ''The state of our dear little sick sister is always the same. I do not think that the end is as near as we had thought at first. This angel will remain with us for a few months yet to edify us and prepare us for her departure. She was telling me a while ago with almost a worried look: 'Alas! if I should be well again?' I quickly reassured her that there was no hope as far as I could see. Entertain yourself as much as possible at the Musse, that is all your little daughter wishes and, indeed, why should you be sad because she is leaving us when this is a source of so much joy for her. She is facing death as a most lovable messenger. It is even odd and amusing to hear her, she happily sees herself growing thin: 'How happy I am,' she says while looking at her hands, 'how the sight of my wasting away delights me.' ''

We are here in a total paradox: what should make her sad gives her joy and, more baffling yet, what should make her happy finds no echo in her heart. The perspective of the delights beyond, the joys of heaven, as we say, stir no echoes in her when her sister recalls them. Besides, she admits, that for some time, she has not known what a great joy is nor even experienced the desire to have any! What draws her is something else, not the perspective of her own happiness but a yet greater experience of love. In the middle of this admirable letter, there is this sentence of flawless spiritual density: ''I think only of the love I shall receive and of the love I shall be able to give.''[12]

7. *WITNESSES OF THE SHADOW*

This second blessing of the shadow thus consists in making what would appear absolutely incompatible come together. Thérèse of the Child Jesus manages to do that easily during the summer of 1897 when God is purifying her in view of her eternal destiny which begins on September 30, the day when she definitely enters into life. It is within the Holy Family that she draws her profound inspiration.

In these same months of 1897, another exceptional character, Charles de Foucauld, having no apparent connection with the young Thérèse Martin, is also going to expereince and understand that his roots in the Holy Family are the key to his life.

A small incident, which takes place a few days after the letter we have just quoted, reveals the world in which St. Thérèse was living toward the end of her life.

This was in July 1897. Someone had sent the sick sister some luscious fruit which she could not eat. She would take them each in turn in her hands as if she wished to offer them to someone.

"The Holy Family has been well served," she said. "St. Joseph and the Child Jesus each had a peach and two plums."

Then, she experienced qualms of scruples, very much in keeping with the times and the education she had received, a kind of uneasiness brought on by the pleasure of seeing and touching these peaches. Her sister reassured her.

Thérèse went on explaining the innermost thoughts of her soul: "The Blessed Virgin also had her share. When I am given some milk with rum in it, I offer it to St. Joseph; I say to myself: Oh! how good this will be for poor Joseph! In the refectory, I always watched to whom I should give each dish. The sweet was for the Child Jesus, the strong for St. Joseph. The Blessed Virgin was not forgotten either. But when there was something missing, when someone forgot to pass the salad dressing, I was much happier because it seemed to me that I was definitely giving something away to the Holy Family, being really deprived of what I was offering."[13]

At about this time, when the missionaries with whom she was corresponding (as long as she was still able to write) asked her to choose a baptismal name for a young catechumen, she would always slip in the name of Joseph along with another name. In her last summer she would throw flowers at his statue at the bottom of the chestnut lane.[14] All this may appear childish. It is simply clever, when we sense that these humble practices could help her overcome atrocious suffering, spiritual as well as physical, and by the very fact, create the peace of heart and selfless love which is the secret of the Carmel, and therefore of the Holy Family, and of the Holy Spirit. It is the triumph of the coincidence of contradictories.

At precisely the same time, Charles de Foucauld turned to the world of Joseph on March 10, 1897, and he was perfectly aware that this was on a Wednesday of the month of St. Joseph: "The first Wednesday I spent there (in Nazareth), you made me enter, my God, as a servant of the St. Clare Convent through the intercession of St. Joseph."[15]

A whole life, incredibly eventful, finds its definite direction at last. For a long time, God had managed to reach him, through Africa, the desert, Teresa of Avila whose teaching he diligently put into practice, Father Huvelin, his dear cousin Marie de Bondy, his stay at the Trappist monastery after his conversion in 1886: everything converged toward Nazareth, the land of Joseph, his protector, as well as the land of Jesus. He felt irresistibly called to this land.

First he sought Nazareth in the strict enclosure of the Poor Clares at the time when the young Carmelite of twenty-four years, St. Thérèse, was yielding her marvellous destiny to the Church. Then he sought it with increasing intensity in the brotherhood of Beni-Abbès which preserved some vestiges of enclosure as it did not wish to be a hermitage cut off from the world, but a *zaouia*, a brotherhood like Joseph's modest dwelling in Nazareth.

A whole series of changes will take him to the impressive panorama of the Hoggar at Tamanrasset in North Africa. There, all the remains of an enclosure have disappeared: all that is left is the enclosure of the heart, so interior that he no longer even calls himself Charles of Jesus, as he had previously, but only Charles, his baptismal name which contains everything like the name of Jesus, at the origin of Mary's name, at the origin of the name of Joseph, the one who will give a name to Jesus, "for there is no other name under heaven given among mortals by which we must be saved" (Ac 4:12).

"My vocation, identified so many times, is life in Nazareth," he writes to Father Huvelin on April 4, 1905. In short, he gradually realizes the admirable definition of the Holy Family given by Father Huvelin, in a letter of August 2, 1896: "Nazareth, that is, where one works, where one obeys . . . it is a house one builds in one's heart, or rather a house that one allows to be built in oneself by Jesus' hands." Now we know these two hands Jesus uses to create the true atmosphere of the Holy Spirit who, himself, builds the Church: they are Joseph and Mary.

ANNEX: *A NEW SPIRITUAL SPACE*

Why does Charles de Foucauld no longer need the slightest enclosure at the end of his life and simply calls himself Charles? Because, at last, on this earth of man, he totally belongs to the new spiritual space where our baptismal name, through the power of the blood of Christ, takes on an undreamt-of relief. The greatest powers, the most formidable possibilities are less important than it: "Do not rejoice at this, that the spirits submit to you," says the Lord to his astonished apostles, "but rejoice that your names are written in heaven" (Lk 10:20). Charles de Foucauld had been introduced by Joseph, on Wednesday, March 10, 1897, into this space that the eternal Father had entrusted to him. He never ceased to immerse himself in it with delight.

No one has better described this than another Charles, Charles Péguy in his little posthumous masterpiece, *Véronique ou Dialogue de l'histoire avec l'âme charnelle*: "There are two halves, so to speak, in this mechanism. One of the halves is infinite and in itself, as it were, eternal. The other of the two halves is infinitesimal and in itself, as it were, temporal. And what is most striking, by a new miracle, the infinitesimal part is no less necessary, no less indispensable to the whole, to the adjustment of the whole, than the infinite part, being exactly, precisely, by a singular twist, necessary, itself indispensable to this infinite part. Thus to deny one or the other part is also to deny the whole, to dismantle the marvellous device. A God. A God-man. But to deny heaven is almost certainly not dangerous. It is a heresy without a future. It is so obviously crude. To deny the earth, on the contrary, is enticing. First, to do so is refined. Which is the worst. Thus, the dangerous heresy is there, the heresy with a future. . . ."[16]

It is the heresy of those who seek the fullness of truth outside the Holy Family: if they are truly intelligent and humble, they will discover this mysterious star ("the shadow of the Father") which guides them to the Child and Mary his mother; most often, they go astray in pursuit of the gurus' woolly theories, toward disastrous imitations where one professes to scorn the earth the better to find heaven.

The wonderful world of Joseph! No one, undoubtedly, has defined it better than the favorite daughter of St. Teresa of Avila, Anne of St. Bartholomew,[17] who gathered the secrets of her thinking. She describes this world to Bérulle in 1609, a world we must all find:

"As far as my soul is concerned, I keep it in peace in his presence and in a profound silence. Through the kindness of God, I have found again some of the graces he used to give me at other times, but I am more unfaithful than ever, more unworthy of these graces. This serene presence reduces movement and passions to subjection and, so to speak, to death. And even if, at times, some fugitive thought or some movement rises, this view of God immediately puts them to silence leaving nothing for me to do. And I have no other desire but this: that his will be done in little things and in great ones. In a particularly enlightened moment, the Lord showed me, one day, during a moment of recollection, that neither in heaven nor on earth can the soul have greater happiness than to be in agreement with his will. Tell me if this is good."

One will appreciate, on the one hand, the inspiration, and on the other, the humility. This letter goes on and continues to describe this discovery which is no other than what we have called the mystery of the fourth Mansion, that is the passage of what remains very human to what becomes other, so new in its simplicity that one cannot describe it. "We do not know what it is." "It is not something we can savor but a force of truth: God shows (the soul) the differences there are between the action of God and the natural operations." God makes one see that the latter move toward enslavement, while the others lead to the discovery of liberty, of fidelity of the spirit.

Then follows an interesting note: "The soul scorns all things that are not God and yet it finds it masters them. This scorn does not cast human things aside but, on the contrary, leans on them while granting them their true place."

Then comes a delightful sentence expressing a great truth: whatever be the stage of spiritual life we reach on earth, we must constantly live the death of the kernel of wheat, this humble break which we sense to be the specialty of the "patron saint of a happy death." We can say that this experience gradually becomes easier: "Even if this meditative prayer does not always remain in this state, the humility it introduces into the actions it performs subsists in the soul almost as if the prayer was going on."[18]

Is that not, already on earth, this other world of which Mary spoke to Bernadette on February 18, 1858 where we may begin,

118   *St. Joseph: Shadow of the Father*

thanks to her and to her husband, "to be happy" in a style much different from the usual joys of this earth?

1 It is worthwhile to refer to the Jewish exegesis concerning Joseph; for example, *Un Messie nommé Joseph* by Josy Eisenberg and Benno Gross, Albin Michel, 1983.

2 The author of Ecclesiasticus is also struck by the influence of these bones (cf Si 48:10, 15).

3 All these patterns of thought are, in certain aspects, linked with an aging St. Augustine. Cf the excellent remarks by J. Ansaldi in the *Dictionnaire de Spiritualité*, XII, p. 432.

4 *The Complete Works of St. Teresa of Jesus*, op. cit., *Interior Castle*, 6th Mansion, ch. 9, p. 319.

5 A profoundly sound thesis defended by André Glucksmann in his book *La bêtise*.

6 *De l'Actualité Historique*, DDB, 1960, vol. 1, p. 188 ff. The study as a whole is one of rare depth.

7 It is known that Freud considered sadomasochism to be one of the most widespread and most important perversions. It is a form of inversion.

8 Dante, *The Divine Comedy*, Carlyle Wicksteed translation, Modern Library, New York, 1932, Paradise, canto XXXIII, lines 1-3.

9 It is the intuition that "matures" when we reflect upon what God has willed in the Holy Family. It is found in a text by Msgr. Richaud (*L'Aquitaine*, 14 December 1962), a text which comments on John XXIII's decision about Joseph's place in the canon of the Mass.

10 *Autour de la docte ignorance* (1450), trans. Van Steenberghe, p. 40. Nicholas of Cusa (1401-1464) played an important role as adviser to the Holy See and as a diplomat. His culture was vast and his insights astonishing. The principle he states here, on the spiritual level, is oddly enough applied to modern physics where "all the experiments, without any exception, demand two contradictory principles to be explained or, rather, a principle supposing the superimposing of two principles each excluding the other." A. Michel, *France Catholique*, 15 June 1984.

11 This wording is used by *The New American Bible*, revised ed. 1986.

12 *Derniers entretiens*, DDB, pp. 707-708.

13 *Ibid.*, p. 277.

14 *Ibid.*

15 J.F. Six, *Itinéraire spirituel de Charles de Foucauld*, p. 196.

16 C. Péguy, *Oeuvres en prose*, 1909-1914, La Pléiade, p. 392.

17 Anne of St. Bartholomew, a simple and profound soul, had, like St. Teresa, a kind of basic affinity with St. Joseph.

18 Cf Sérouet, *Anne de Saint Barthélémy. Lettres et écrits spirituels*, DDB, 1964, p. 76.

CHAPTER VI

The Time of the Father

1. TIME, A PATERNAL MYSTERY

LET us begin the sixth stage of our journey, an essential one: the art of making the most of time. Jesus, in Nazareth, made use of time as the young Samuel had in the past in the temple of God (cf 1 S 2:26); he "increased in wisdom and in years, and in divine and human favor" (Lk 2:52).

Such is perfection: making use of a time that integrates the least human effort with great divine favor. A time that brings about growth, a time that builds for eternity. A time in which nothing goes to waste.

It is impossible to say what time is. "What, then, is time?" St. Augustine would ask. "If no one ask of me, I know; if I wish to explain to him who asks, I know not."[1] We can say that time is as difficult to know as is the Father: all human reality unfolds in it, it accompanies us always. All reality comes from the Father who is "always at work," as Jesus says, who never leaves us on our own. It is not therefore a matter of explaining it but of making the most of it as Jesus did in Joseph's home for so long. As Jesus, "although he was a Son," wanted to learn to do in strict obedience (cf Heb 5:8).

Jesus acknowledges that time is the Father's business, he

knows that his words will not pass away while heaven and earth will pass away — but he does not know when. "About that day or hour no one knows, neither the angels in heaven, nor the Son, but only the Father" (Mk 13:32). This concealment, bound as always to a kind of ongoing revelation, is proper to Joseph. A disciple of Mary's like Monsieur Olier, so inspired, knew that very well: "He was the oracle of Jesus Christ that made him know every will of the Father in heaven; he was the timekeeper that showed him all the earmarked moments in God's decrees; it was before this oratory that, speaking to his Father, he would say 'Our Father' and invoke him for the whole Church."

Indeed, for thirty years out of thirty-three, ten elevenths of his life, Jesus seemed to depend solely on him as if this slow process of becoming mature entrusted to his hands was the secret of his profound formation.

It is in Joseph that the time of the Father is planned, that is, the time spent on earth by the Heart of the Son fulfilling a very precise twofold purpose: to reveal the true face of God "our Father" (cf Ep 1:2) and "to overthrow" the enemy, "the Prince of this world" (cf Jn 12:31), as the prayer "Our Father" states clearly.

The life of the Holy Family is entirely focused on this twofold ultimate purpose by the virtue of the blood of Christ: Joseph, the "righteous" man, will progressively reflect justice, that is, the holiness of God, and Mary his mercy. Both, in humility, will help the eternal Son in his struggle against evil. Mary is the one who, when he reaches the age of twelve, the important stage in his life when he has outgrown his childhood, will lead him away from the temple to Nazareth and have him choose this father whom God is pointing to him. When he reaches thirty, the age of heavy responsibilities, she is again the one who seems to show him his hour, the hour of the confrontation with the Prince of this world, the hour of the first miracle which singles him out not only before men, who will begin to believe in him, but before the spirits. And Jesus, in St. John, finds himself again in the temple but in a temple which has become a den of thieves where his parents will no longer come to fetch him.

Spiritually speaking, Joseph does not leave him, given the mysterious bond which has gradually woven itself between the eternal Father and himself: "The one who sent me is with me; he has not left me alone, for I always do what is pleasing to him" (Jn 8:29). But humanly speaking, this poor and wonderful father on earth has completed his task. Putting what he has slowly learned to good use, Jesus will defy the enemy by the Spirit of God: "If it is by the Spirit of God that I cast out demons, then the kingdom of God has come to you" (Mt 12:21).

Jesus denounces Satan at work everywhere: among the Pharisees who believe they are the sons of Moses while they are doing the enemy's work: "You are from your father the Devil, and you choose to do your father's desires" (Jn 8:44); among his own friends, Peter and Judas. He banishes him from many bodies where he has taken abode. But the most extraordinary battle that Jesus will wage against him will be carried out exactly in the style of his father Joseph: totally hidden, totally incomprehensible, when seen from the outside. It will consist in surrendering himself to the stupid and criminal inventions of diabolical perversity, translating itself into the desperate mad rage of radical injustice, for it is exercised against the only perfectly innocent being the earth has ever borne. This is what St. John describes as having "loved to the end" (Jn 13:1)

The Devil cannot understand anything about this love, its consistency, its efficacy, a love destined to shatter the falsified human prudence, the conniving human justice (without which the Devil would be helpless) and all the criminal idiocies invented by men in the name of a certain social order.[2] On the third day, life crushes death, when the latter thought its triumph was definitive.

Joseph had long prepared Jesus for this confrontation, by using a strategy which we will attempt to examine more closely in the final stage of our journey.

One of the undeniable aspects of this strategy is the art of waiting for the favorable moment, like the hunter on the watch, and also the art of abiding. Jesus seemed to want to begin his Messianic career at the age of twelve or, at least, to begin a kind of official career. He will have to wait in total self-effacement until he is thirty. "A self-effacement forever incomprehensible . . ." as Bossuet would say, more shocking than death itself, investing him with an astonishing greatness of the kind that can impress a pagan like the centurion. From the human point of view there is nothing in Nazareth. In reality, time takes on its full significance, its total density: there one learns to perfection the art of waiting for the favorable moment and to abiding, both being, as it were, the temporal version of "the narrow gate found by very few" and of "the narrow path which leads to life."

Joseph sets the example: he does what the angel tells him, whatever the hour or circumstances. He fulfils his particular duty to the end.

Jesus takes advantage of every moment to obey, to learn, to grow in every sense of the word, humanly and spiritually, before God and before men. Some day, he will translate this experience of Nazareth and of eternal life, on earth as in heaven: "My Father is still working, and I also am working" (Jn 5:17). Besides, when we learn to live there (this is the whole meaning of the effort made in this reflection which is also an action), we become very much aware that, whatever may happen, pain or joy, success or failure, dryness or consolation, we are building by the grace of God, we are making progress. Time becomes grace and since time never fails us, grace never fails us. The Father can, somehow or other, reach the Son in us.

To live within the Holy Family is therefore gradually to learn who the Father is and, by the same token, to fight against evil, that is against whatever prevents one from seeing the Father, against whatever distorts or even perverts his image. The silent Joseph, the one responsible for this image, places before our eyes this maxim from St. John of the Cross: "If thou desirest to attain to holy recollection, thou shalt attain it, not by admitting, but by refusing."[3] This is the secret of the good use of time. What does this mean?

Like the unfortunate Pilate, we never know what the truth is. It is too beautiful, too vast, too simple, too new for us. It would frighten us. We are not worthy of it. Joseph did not feel he was worthy of Mary and of what she was bearing.

On the other hand, everywhere there are obtrusive people, dangerous imitators disguised as shepherds or Herod's soldiers whom one must avoid.

The principal art of the use of time is to be able to put aside what is false, corrupt, inexact, unworthy, fuzzy. The one who approaches Mary, like Joseph, does not allow himself to be seduced so easily. That was the case for Bernadette: the most enticing beauties of Lourdes, in this brilliant Second Empire, did not bear comparison, "they cannot compare with her!"

Thus, without knowing too well how, by casting aside the false we move toward the true. It happened that, at the end of the sixteenth century, the German astronomer Kepler, penniless, without instruments, at grips with the war and cruel family difficulties, made stunning discoveries. It had always been believed that the course of heavenly bodies was circular. But, in that case, a small angle in the revolution of the planet Mars remained unaccountable. Meticulous observations had brought this to attention.

Because of this small angle, Kepler did research for some twenty years, convinced that the Creator must have had a harmonious solution to the problem which absorbed him. At last, at the very beginning of the seventeenth century, he discovered that the planets follow an elliptical course. His joy was boundless as if he had probed the secrets of God, the same kind of joy we experience ourselves when we enter a little further into the world of Joseph, into the secrets of the Father.

The more we abide with them, Jesus, Mary, Joseph, the less the idols, small or great, will be able to satisfy us; the more deceit, in all its forms, will inspire horror in us, the more we will manage to sense that the poverty of the first beatitude is the key to true possession.

We have come to the sixth stage of our journey, the one where we must learn to abide. How can one not think of the sixth Mansion of the *Interior Castle*?

Indeed, as we reflect on this Mansion, the longest one, the most important one after the necessary journey through the fourth, the final preparation for the seventh, the last one, I beg the angels and the saints to come to my aid. To make the most of the time spent with Joseph, as Jesus gave us such a powerful example, is the condition to enter into contemplation with Mary. Every sin is a distraction, it makes us abandon the way, it regrettably takes possession of something of our inner perception, of our vital energy, of our soul. Mary is the totally attentive woman, for the focus of her whole being is centered solely on Christ, her child and her God. To experience time with Joseph is to learn to go from distraction to attention. An endless task! That is why the demands of the sixth stage are so great. That is why Joseph is so helpful.

2. THE MAN OF WEDNESDAY

Wednesday, the fourth day of the Jewish week from which the Christian week was copied, is the middle day, the day finally attributed to Joseph by a tradition which slowly emerged through the centuries. If we contemplate the seven-branched candelabra, a symbol of the divine action abounding from the Holy Spirit, we see that it rests on a base which is an extension of the fourth branch, the middle one around which the others counterpoise each other. Symbolically, this consideration expresses a reality as hidden as it is powerful: Joseph is the one the Father wanted to make responsible for the success of Jesus' coming and formation, of the descent of eternity into time.

In face of this inconceivable descent, Péguy is amazed: ". . . the technique of Christianity, the technique and the mechanism of its mystique, of the Christian mystique, that is what it is: it is putting one mechanical part in gear with another; it is the interlocking of two parts, this remarkable commitment, mutual, unique, reciprocal, impossible to undo: that cannot be taken apart; of the first into the second and of the second into the first; of the temporal into the eternal, and (but especially, what is most often denied, what is in fact most amazing), of the eternal into the temporal."[4] It is in the house of Joseph, in his hands, in his arms that this commitment takes place. That is why it is eminently proper that he should be the man of Wednesday, of the day on which, in such an unexpected way in Genesis, the author brings time into being.

The time of humanity begins on the fourth day with the creation of the sun and the moon, and the stars which are barely mentioned. Strictly speaking, we modestly call them "the great luminaries," for they are so beautiful, so omnipresent, so essential to the life of man, night and day, that the danger of worshipping them was great, as other nations proved. In fact, the service expected of them, in addition to their irreplaceable light and warmth of life, is to measure time. The sun sees to the year, which it regulates by means of the seasons, "a marvellous instrument it is, the work of the Most High" (Si 43:2). Psalm 19 describes its resplendent rise, "it comes out like a bridegroom from his wedding canopy" (Ps 19:5). As for the moon, it measures the months with a fidelity that filled the ancients with admiration:

> He made the moon, to serve in its season
> to mark the times and to be an everlasting sign.
> From the moon comes the sign for feast days,
> a light that waves when it has reached the full (Si 43:6-7).[5]

The stars serve as a decor, as a framework for these movements and as points of reference.

Now, what do we see in Genesis? Joseph, the son of Jacob at the age of seventeen, dreams that while working in a field, he sees sheaves that he and his brothers are gathering. "His sheaf rises and stands upright; then his brothers' sheaves gather around it, and bow down to his sheaf" (cf Gn 37:7). A prophetic dream which will come true: it is the homage of the earth that this great character will receive in Egypt.

But this dream is but an introduction to the homage of heaven: "Look, I have had another dream: the sun, the moon, and eleven stars were bowing down to me" (Gn 37:9). The heavenly bodies which mark out time are bowing before this man, chosen to save his people and introduce the mysterious "savior of the Savior," whose greatness is equalled only by his humble self-effacement.

The Jewish reflection called Midrash creates a most interesting maxim about dreams:

> The dreams of the evildoers
> are neither from heaven nor from the earth,
> but the dreams of the just
> are of both, heaven and earth (*Tan'houna*).[6]

This means that the evildoers and their dreams belong to this unhappy "in-between" space, which is neither heaven nor earth, the neither yes nor no space that Jesus denounces as the domain of the evil one. The one called "righteous" by contrast, dwells with the righteous Joseph in this spiritual Nazareth where precisely heaven and earth meet, the earth introducing heaven, the human temporal becoming the support for the eternal. That is the secret of time as experienced in Joseph: but even if at times it is like a journey through the desert, even if it appears trying, negative from the human point of view, faith assures us that it builds. The more we believe this, the truer it is, for the Father can refuse nothing to this son who fights according to rules, like the athlete in a sports competition or the farmer who labors (cf 2 Tm 2:5-6). "If we endure, we will also reign with him" (2 Tm 2:12).

The reference to the eleven stars in this dream is also significant. The stars recall the humble beginnings of the Church. Humble but fundamental, for it is the Church of the Eleven that celebrated the Last Supper, heard the admirable admonitions which followed, were witnesses to the death and the resurrection of the Savior, met the Risen One, were present at his glorious ascension, prepared the Pentecost. A certain Joseph, called the Just, was approached to bring the number in the college of the apostles up to twelve, the number of the Church — but no, he was set aside in favor of Matthias. Joseph appears again, like a fugitive cloud, and disappears (cf Ac 1:23).

3. THE FULLNESS OF TIME

One thing is certain and its proportions are unfathomable. It is in the arms of Joseph that history reached what St. Paul calls "the fullness of time" (Gal 4:4). What is the fullness of time? It is the coming toward which the whole effort of creation is directed, toward which the whole effort of history is reaching out, while humans are generally unaware of it (the saints alone are!): to give sons to the Father. The very sign of this coming is to be able to call the Father *Abba*, Daddy, something the Jews cannot do for the time being. The history of the Chosen People is a slow ascent toward this coming of which the arms of Joseph were the witnesesses, "these arms in which Jesus found so much delight," as St. Francis de Sales says.

The tragedy of human existence is that men are the slaves of dark forces, as St. Paul says, and that they acquire the mentality of a slave which perverts everything, even the Law. The Law is good: it is made to free individuals from their inner chains and, by the very fact, the whole social body has its life made tolerable. Society will no longer be this cut-throat, this closed-in area of constant settlement of scores, of pillage, and of sterile confrontations. Alas! The Law which was to act as a canopy of love has itself become a chain, underscoring the weakness and folly of humans, further increasing the enslavement of poor humanity. It is the heart-breaking declaration in the Letter to the Romans — before the filial Spirit of Jesus, fruit of the blood shed out of love, comes at last to unsettle all things and restore the secret of the beginning to humanity.

The prophets, it is true, with the light of the Spirit, had anticipated all those wonders. Jeremiah, in a special way, draws tears by his wait, both despairing and perfectly assured of having a true paternal protection. What should be said of Hosea in chapter 11? of Isaiah in chapter 54? "For a brief moment I abandoned you, but with great compassion I will gather you. In overflowing wrath for a moment I hid my face from you, but with everlasting love I will have compassion on you" (Is 54:7-8).

Unfortunately, eyes do not see and ears do not hear for a relatively simple reason: the concentration of forces which correspond to true attention is disorganized. The centers of interest are elsewhere, the eyes of the soul are, as it were, out of focus, the vital force is absorbed by other things. Let one simply observe how anxiety, for example, can alienate, in the proper sense of the word ("make one other than he is himself"), a human being even if he is intelligent, generous, well-bred. What should be said about base passions like jealousy, hatred, the instinct of domination, despair, fear?

Having come to the end of its long journey, the community of the sons of Israel has all the elements necessary to discover that God is a father and that, at all cost, he wants to be considered as such in order at last to manifest himself that he is so. The Book of Wisdom testifies to this, the last book of the Old Law: "It is your providence, O Father, that steers the vessel in its course in the sea!'' (cf Ws 14:3). But it holds on to its slave mentality. The Son himself has to come and experience something altogether different in its midst. ''While we were minors, we were enslaved to the elemental spirits of the world. But when the fullness of time had come, God sent his Son, born of a woman, born under the law, in order to redeem those who were under the law, so that we might receive adoption as children. And because you are children, God has sent the Spirit of his Son into our hearts, crying, Abba! Father! So you are no longer a slave but a child, and if a child then also an heir, through God'' (Gal 4:3-7).

For those who are beginning to understand, the Spirit makes them choose instinctively suggesting from within[7] what the Law was authoritatively suggesting from without: the difference is radical. This coming is what constitutes the fullness of time.

One understands that a mind as enlightened as that of St. Francis de Sales could have had an intuitive understanding of the complete newness of what the affectionate trust of Jesus in Joseph's arms was suggesting: ''I cannot imagine anything sweeter than to see this heavenly little Jesus in the arms of this great saint, calling him Daddy thousands of times in his childish talk and with a totally loving and filial heart'' (Letter to Monsignor Camus, March 1609). It was this vision of the tiny Jesus in the arms of Joseph wearing a red cloak that brought an end to the one hundred and fifty-three days (the number of the last miraculous catch of fish in St. John) of apparitions in Fatima, as if to point to a much greater climax than ''the dance of the sun,'' in spite of the impact it made on the minds of the people.

Jesus tells us: ''Truly I tell you, unless you change and become like children, you will never enter the kingdom of heaven'' (Mt 18:3). How will we be able to take such a route?

It is here that the coincidence of contradictories reaches a kind of climax: to make the most of time in Joseph's home (when we have learned to do so!), does not mean to grow old, to become hardened, to steel ourselves with habits and elements of knowledge, but it is to be rejuvenated, to become more flexible, to free ourselves from clutter and to become simple. This is the whole journey taken by Thérèse of the Child Jesus on which a great contemporary theologian meditates: ''It is one of the wonders of the relationship with God that maturity and the spirit of childhood grow at the same pace.''[8]

Basically, as we reflect on this, we follow in time the road which is exactly the inverse to that of Jesus: Jesus starts from Christmas, a mysterious union of heaven and earth, where angels and men appear united as they never will be again, and he journeys on to his baptism. This baptism, slowly prepared by Joseph, takes on a completely significant aspect: the descent into the waters of the Jordan along with sinners is the image of the death of Jesus; the climbing out is the image of the resurrection and the blessing of the Father with the presence of the Spirit, the image of Pentecost. The three years of public life are only the unfolding of this baptism: ''I came to bring fire to the earth, and how I wish it were already kindled! I have a baptism with which to be baptized, and what stress I am under until it is completed!'' (Lk 12:49-50). Jesus works for the fire of the Spirit of which the condition is the waters of death.

Jesus went to the end of his mission: he faced his death in all its brutality with the meekness of ''the lamb that is led to the slaughter, and like a sheep that before its shearers is silent . . .'' (Is 53:7). ''Upon him was the punishment that made us whole, and by his bruises we are healed'' (Is 53:5).

We, on the contrary, in the immeasurable mercy of God, start from baptism where we die, we rise again with Jesus where we receive ''his Spirit in our hearts as a first installment'' (2 Cor 1:22): the door through which Jesus makes his exit becomes the entrance door for us. Jesus leaves the Holy Family through his baptism to enable us to enter there through ours (which is still his). Thus we are entitled to have Mary as mother and, through her, Joseph as father. We can move toward childhood, toward Christmas, toward the fullness of time. Our death should be the *dies natalis* of the ancients, the day of our birth to eternal life. An astonishing inversion! An incomprehensible movement of time! An overwhelming experience!

Thus if, with the Holy Family, we make the most of this poor shuffling human existence, so trite, so dull, with its perspectives sometimes opening out to such dead-ends, it will make us move toward "the beginning." "The beginning" is the world of the Father that Jesus comes to restore so that some day he will be able to hand it over into his hands. Some day, indeed, "the end will come, when he hands over the kingdom to God the Father," after having destroyed all the powers of the enemy, the last one being death (cf 1 Cor 15:24).

Like the Jordan, whose waters flowed back to their source when the Hebrews crossed it on their way to the promised land (cf Ps 114:3), the time spent at Joseph's house moves toward the beginning. Otherwise, it moves toward nothingness — unless one is converted. Yes, to enter into the Holy Family by living one's baptism is to walk in the night of faith toward the light of Christmas. It is to begin to know the secret joy promised by Mary to the little Bernadette, on February 18, 1858, the joy of "the other world" in the midst of this one.

4. SPACE AND TIME

Time never leaves us — but now that the angels are beginning to show us Joseph's face as that of the Father (undoubtedly, because we have become a little more like children!), the demands on our attention are doubled. It is no longer a question of living by chance, of letting ourselves go according to our whims, no matter how; we must, like Jesus and in him, be on the watch for what the Father says to us through him, in this constantly renewed reality which presents him, this reality which makes us move forward

"from beginnings to beginnings up to the eternal beginning,"
according to the admirable words of St. Gregory of Nyssa.

One could think that this is painful, that it is the end to all
spontaneity and that, because we must turn our backs to Egypt, to
its enticements, its universal slavery, we are "condemned to liberty," as Jean-Paul Sartre would say. Besides, St. Paul says
something of the kind: "having been set free from sin, [you] have
become slaves of righteousness" (Rm 6:18), the slaves of truth.
But he adds that this is a totally human way of speaking, adapted to
our distorted mentality. To be a slave of sin is to be a slave of
illusion; it is to move toward sterility, destruction, disgust, the
void. To be slave of holiness is to be rejuvenated, to breathe, to
move toward a kind of symphony where everything speaks, where
everything communicates. It is to live on earth this new time which
Jesus explains to the Samaritan woman: "The hour is coming and
is now here, when the true worshippers will worship the Father in
spirit and in truth" (Jn 4:23).

In a word, it means to enter into this secret garden, the Virgin
Mary, where God takes such delight. "She is on earth a sanctuary
that God fills with wonders and in which he wants to take his rest in
a new way. She is a new paradise, not earthly like that of Adam
which was destroyed by his sin, nor heavenly like that of the angels
which exists only in heaven, but she, on earth, is a heavenly
paradise that God has planted with his own hand and that her angel
keeps for the Second Adam, for the king of heaven and earth who
must live there. But that is hidden to our eyes. . . ."[9] Everything is
hidden by Joseph, everything is buried in the secret of this son of
David who is the one responsible for and the protector of this space
(cf Mt 1:20), where men redeemed by the blood of Christ must
learn to become sons in the Son, kings of heaven and earth. If Mary
is the secret of this new space, Joseph is the secret of this new time
which opens the entrance to it. Indeed, what characterizes the
Marian space is a superior quality of attention, the loving contemplation which is the masterpiece of the Holy Spirit; what makes this

attention possible is the art of slipping into time on reality, like the bird on the air, by taking the whole reality into account, without allowing ourselves to get engulfed or perturbed by anything. What an art! All the realism and all the detachment of Joseph is necessary for that.

This space and this time, so new, so humble and so great, constitute the true Jerusalem where everything must be fulfilled:

> I will pay my vows to the Lord,
> in the presence of all his people,
> in the courts of the house of the Lord,
> in your midst, O Jerusalem (Ps 116:18-19).

We are no longer speaking about a geographical city, as Jesus points out to the Samaritan woman, but about a spiritual city of which Nazareth was and can still be the reality today, if we wish. Nazareth in Galilee, in the northern part of the country, in the area that is scorned because it is impregnated with pagan influences, that is exactly where the risen Son must manifest himself: "You are looking for Jesus of Nazareth, who was crucified? He has been raised; he is not here [in Jerusalem] . . . . But go, tell his disciples and Peter that he is going ahead of you to Galilee; there you will see him, just as he told you" (Mk 16:6-7). Words of angels, words of God!

"With what can we compare the kingdom of God?" (Mk 4:30) Jesus was asking himself while thinking of the ones speaking to him. How can one speak of the subject which holds our interest? How can one make someone understand realities which, in fact, are very simple and very real? The mystery of Christ intimately comes through Joseph and Mary as the mystery of human existence unfolds itself in space and time. These truths reveal themselves only through experience. Contrary to what one might think, there is nothing intellectual about them. It is a matter of experiencing time with Jesus as an act of obedience to the Father and, for that, one must let oneself be begotten by the Spirit "in the shadow of the holy marriage." Mary makes us become attentive to the reality of which she has the secret and Joseph creates these conditions of peace, of detachment, of faith in Christ and most especially of patience, absolutely necessary for the action of God.

God needs time and especially a time of silence (what St. John of the Cross calls *callado amor*, silent love) to do his work. This is obvious in the episode of the adulteress: before these men, whose unleashed fury drives them to stone this woman, Jesus calmly writes in the sand, without a word, as if simply to gain time. Effectively, everything will topple over in an unexpected way in these hardened hearts. Jesus gives himself great moments of solitary prayer at night after his forty-day retreat in the desert.

All this is the fruit of this very long period of learning about the time of the Father that Jesus must undergo with Joseph in Nazareth. He, who is so great, in contrast with his fellow citizens of Galilee, in no way feels that he is the master of this time: "My time has not yet come, but your time is always here. The world cannot hate you, but it hates me because I testify against it that its works are evil" (Jn 7:6-7). The time of the Father is a present, forever new, unprecedented, demanding, from which one must not escape by indulging in day-dreaming, useless memories, unbridled imagination, distraction. There is nothing more rigorous, nothing more important.

Jesus learned it through Joseph and Mary who learned everything, in their turn, by meditating on the surprising reactions of the one they were discovering more and more: they had been so amazed by the prophecies they had heard about him in the temple when he was small (cf Lk 2:23). They had understood nothing in his reply at the time of his famous escapade at the temple when he was twelve!

How could we ever really learn about the time of the Father without following the roads that Jesus took?

One thing is certain: this time, well spent, leads to a perfection in service and in love: "Now before the festival of the Passover, Jesus knew that his hour had come to depart from this world and go to the Father. Having loved his own who were in the world, he loved them to the end" (Jn 13:1). and John points to Jesus "who, knowing that the Father has placed all things in his hands," humbly washes the apostles' feet like a slave as if an action of this kind perfectly characterized the world of the Father, the world translated by Joseph. The conclusion is clear: "you also ought to wash one another's feet" (Jn 13:14).

5. DIVINE MAGIC

This scene taken from St. John sets the tone for what we could call "divine magic," the divine art of making everything work together for such humble love, like in a symphony where, in an almost magic way, everything — sounds, timbres, rhythms, clever convolution — contributes to create simple beauty. This divine magic drew amazement from Einstein as he thought of the gigantic chaos of the phenomena of nature, observed by physics, ultimately translating itself into very simple laws, coherent and harmonious.

Divine magic is exactly the opposite of human magic, often inspired by the Devil, against which the Bible severely warns us.

The latter is focused on the search for knowledge and therefore for power with the purpose of enslaving and crushing others in order to impose upon them the questionable superiority of some individual. That is the reason why some high-ranked people of this world have had recourse to it, from the impious Jezebel in the Book of Kings to Hitler, as well as some unhappy wayward individuals who want to be reassured, to take revenge, to appease their passions.

Divine magic, by contrast, is directed toward the service of the poor in a most humble self-effacement. Its motto, based on complete trust in Providence, is given in the Letter to the Romans: "All things work together for good for those who love God, who are called according to his purpose" (Rm 8:28). Everything, absolutely everything, contributes to bring about a favorable change in the heart of the man who experiences time with Joseph, that is, who lives in this very particular climate of humility, flexibility, patience and absolute trust experienced by the saints.

It is the divine magic that clothes the lilies of the fields with splendor, that gives full significance to the hues of sunset, that calls the stars by name, as the prophet says. It is also this divine magic that uses the evil and folly in human beings to carry out astonishing designs where everything is turned about, as we see in the story of the ancient Joseph, sold like a vulgar slave by his brothers and who becomes their savior. St. Paul describes the wonders of this baffling action in himself: "I am content with weakness, insults, hardships, persecutions, and calamities for the sake of Christ; for whenever I am weak, then I am strong" (2 Cor 12:10). The cross of Christ is the triumph of this power of transformation, absolutely beyond our grasp, of the power of the Spirit of love, which will literally explode in the resurrection.

Why call it magic if it designates the opposite of what this word usually describes? Because God is, in fact, the true magician whom others try to ape like the magicians of Pharaoh's court when they were attempting to reproduce the wonders performed by Moses. The Lord uses the forces of nature, events in history, everything that constitutes the usual reality of man to speak to him, to reach him in his heart, to instruct him, to hearten him, to do with each man what the Father does with Jesus in the Gospel. He loves, in contrast to what one might believe, neither visions, nor revelations, nor extraordinary phenomena, nor miracles, notes St. John of the Cross, and "when he works them, he does so, because he cannot do otherwise."[10] The Lord's love for human liberty is too great, he respects it too much to try to fascinate or seduce it.

Unfortunately, very often, humans understand nothing about this language or they even attribute a completely false interpretation to it, like those eminent Jews who wanted to get rid of Jesus supposedly to save the people. In fact, in spite of themselves, they will fulfil the prophecies.

The one who manages to enter into the Holy Family and stay there sees the Father at work in the simplicity of daily existence through the humble Joseph. He does not ask for special signs unless the Lord himself gives them to him as was the case for King Ahaz at the time the virgin gives birth to Emmanuel: "The Lord himself will give you a sign" (Is 7:14).

There simply emerges then such a power of ingenuity, of coherence, of presence, at least from time to time, that one understands the remarkable prophecy made by St. Ignatius of Antioch in the text quoted earlier about the incarnation making all magic disappear. The sun makes the little electric light bulb useless; all the more so does the very simple power of love and truth, when it is allowed to come forth, annihilate the magic powers of deceit and illusion. One understands also why the Magi were drawn in this direction. The star so mysterious, now visible, now invisible, which sets one on one's way but does not exempt one from searching, is the perfect image of what Joseph does in the Church, bringing the alert minds, from whatever direction they may come, to "the child with Mary his mother" (cf Mt 2:11). When we have an inkling of the wonders of the world entrusted to him and of the formation he gives on the part of the Father, we will understand that it is there that God is working out "a plan for the fullness of time, to gather up all things in him [Christ, the one head], things in heaven and things on earth" (Ep 1:10). And it is there and nowhere else that we will want to savor the extraordinary newness of the most modest of our moments.

The story of Bernadette is a remarkable demonstration of what I have called divine magic: from the exceptional poverty of her youth to the no less striking self-effacement of her adult years, everything unfolds in her in an eminently expressive way. Everything conveys the presence in her of "another world."

Besides, the parish priest of Lourdes, not without some astonishment, was aware of this in the spring of 1858: "Everything evolves in her in a striking way!" The words, the gestures, the combination of dates, as we have seen, the fruit she bears, the movements she raises in the midst of Lourdes, which come only from her, the profound spiritual movement of international dimension, everything speaks a language that is not the ordinary language of humans.

Without having done anything out of the ordinary, everything becomes extraordinary in her as it does for whoever knows how to see with the eyes of faith. Without seeing what her eyes have seen, one can see, through her, beyond the usual horizons. One senses what humanity could become, each one of us, if it knew how to find the roads that lead to Nazareth.

ANNEX: *THE STORY OF EMMANUELLE*

The story of Bernadette, the story of Lourdes, yesterday and today, the transfiguration of the ill-famed pig grotto of Lourdes in this Grotto where people from the whole world come to pray, all that perfectly illustrates what the time of the Father can offer when Joseph and Mary find a good plot of soil. What a demonstration of what I have boldly called divine magic! I would like to give a personal example of this, of the kind many could relate. The details of it will, beyond doubt, remain vivid in my memory as long as I live.

It all began during a Mass which was being said in the Pius X Basilica in Lourdes at the beginning of the Eucharistic Congress of 1981. There were some twenty thousand people there. I greeted my neighbor, a tall young man, at the time of the sign of peace. I met him again the following day in my confessional and I recognized him. During the last ceremony, the Ordination Mass attended by close to ninety thousand people, we met again: surprise, exchange of addresses. From then on began a friendly exchange of letters which was soon centered on Our Lady of Life in the Vaucluse where this young man was beginning his training and insisted that I go to visit him.

Two years later, I suddenly decided to take advantage of my February holidays at the seminary of Bayonne to make this trip. Without having planned it so, this journey coincided with February 11, anniversary of the apparitions, a particularly bright day that year. In the vicinity of Lannemezan, while I was reading my pocket-size *Jerusalem Bible* on the train and, especially, the much loved beginning of the third chapter of Colossians, I was swaying as the Jews do when they pray: "If you have been raised with Christ, / seek the things that are above . . . where Christ is seated / at the right hand of God." A young lady of some twenty years, most charming, approached me: "Allow me to?" — "By all means." There were vacant seats everywhere but she wanted this one. "You are reading the Bible?" — "Yes, hear how beautiful it is: 'If you are raised with Christ.' " And I read the whole passage to her.

What followed was as simple as it was unforgettable. She told me the whole story of her life, her attempt at suicide two years before, the little trust she placed in humans, with rare exceptions, one of them being this student in Montpellier she was now going to see. I told her what I was doing in the seminary and, especially, in this month devoted each year to hearing confessions in Lourdes. I spoke to her of Bernadette and of Joseph whom I was in the process of discovering with growing amazement. Much to my surprise, she was keenly interested. She did not grow weary of listening. Luckily, I had with me some farmhouse bread and a good supply of paté to which she did justice. The symbols were there in all their richness.

The conversation went on for hours, without the slightest fatigue. At two in the afternoon, she was calling me by my

Christian name as naturally as Mary used the "vous" with Bernadette. At Montpellier, at about three, she rose to come off the train, leaned over me and hugged me affectionately, making me promise that I would never forget her even if we should never see each other again. I agreed.

How could I forget her? A short while later, as had been agreed, I wrote to her to give her some advice and she wrote back on June 19, 1983 an astonishing letter in which she recalled our "wonderful meeting . . . wonderful, for it is one of the rare moments of my life, of total trust, as if our two lives, our two life-lines, had met and henceforth where to become one line, in total agreement, in complete understanding." At the end of the letter, she was calling me "her little Joseph" and promised she would do everything I would tell her.

On November 9, 1984, I received a letter from her mother. She did not know me but her daughter had spoken much about me and she wanted to let me know what had happened. Emmanuelle had been hit by a lorry while she was riding her motorcycle in southern France, no doubt blinded by the sun. She had died instantly. "Beautiful, not at all disfigured"; it had happened on Wednesday, October 31, at four in the afternoon. How can one not think that Emmanuelle has joined Bernadette and that both of them are now among those we call saints. I am certain they are working with angels, indispensable to make known the most hidden mystery there is, which no human reasoning, no demonstration, can probe, while it is the most irreplaceable and the most useful of all for the moment: that of the fatherhood of Joseph, the condition for Mary's motherhood and the habitual presence of the Spirit of Christ in man. How can one make anyone understand that these three realities are perfectly bound and ordered together?

1 *The Confessions of St. Augustine*, trans. J.G. Pilkington, Liveright Publishing Corp., New York, 1943, XI, 14, 17, p. 285.

2 René Girard has made an authoritative study of these aspects in *Des choses cachées depuis le commencement du monde*, Grasset, 1978.

3 *The Complete Works of Saint John of the Cross*, op. cit., vol. 3, *Spiritual sentences and maxims*, no. 49, p. 224.

4 *Véronique ou Dialogue de l'histoire avec l'âme charnelle*, Oeuvres en prose, 1909-1914, La Pléiade, p. 384.

5 Sirach 43:6, *The New Jerusalem Bible*, 2nd ed., 1985.

6 Cf Josy Eisenberg and Benno Gross, *Un Messie nommé Joseph*, p. 74.

7 This is what St. Thomas Aquinas calls 'instinctus Spiritus Sancti,' the instinct of the Holy Spirit.

8 Hans Urs von Balthasar, *De l'intégration, aspect d'une théologie de l'histoire*, DDB, 1970, p. 108.

9 Bérulle. Translation of a quotation from Régamcy, in *Les plus beaux textes sur la Vierge Marie*, La Colombe, 1946, p. 240.

10 *The Complete Works of St. John of the Cross*, op. cit., vol. 1, *Ascent of Mount Carmel*, III, ch. 31, no. 9, p. 287.

CHAPTER VII

On Being a Son of Joseph

1. AN URGENCY: TO GO DOWN TO NAZARETH

THIS CHAPTER should be simple! But simplicity is a gift, an achievement: work contributes to it without ever having the right to it. Simplicity is a happy encounter between the Creator, both so bountiful and so simple, and his creature whenever the latter consciously assumes its poverty and begins to love him in order to open itself better to divine bounty. Simplicity is Christ himself in whom the Father expresses all things through the Spirit, sums up all things, as St. Paul says, translates all he is by one unique Word.

Mary is the mother of Christ: in 431, the Church acknowledged her as the Mother of God but, not always inspired by divine simplicity or divine humility, men of the Church tend to perceive her on lofty heights. Thérèse of the Child Jesus complains about the fact that Mary is shown as so distant, inaccessible. When Paul VI, on November 21, 1964, proclaimed Mary, Mother of the Church, the Christian people applauded at length. This Mother comes close to us, as she did to Bernadette. If we want her to, she is there, very close, translating the motherhood of the Spirit (the Lourdes pilgrims have a sort of experience of this).

Joseph became the human father of Jesus. The consequences are immeasurable: first, it is in him that the paternity of the unique

Father of Jesus and of all human beings in Jesus came down in a totally original manner: "My Father and your Father, . . . my God and your God . . ." (Jn 20:17), he cries out.

In the same way that the Church has slowly become aware of Mary's motherhood, so she must, little by little, become aware of Joseph's fatherhood, find again the traces of Jesus' obedience, accept the practical exercises of it by going down to Nazareth where divine simplicity is waiting for us. For there is no doubt that Mary, then Joseph, together make up the secret of this simplicity.

One could object that we know nothing about Nazareth since, for profound reasons, Holy Scripture does not speak about it. As for myself, I believe the contrary: everything we were able to make out that was intelligent, all we have been able to experience in the area of friendship, the experience of experiences which was, as it were, the key to the search for truth in one like St. Augustine, in a word, all that is true comes from the Holy Family and goes back to it, leads humans back to it like the Father leads his Son back to it in the Spirit.

One could object that Jesus did not stay on in the Holy Family: our whole meditation attempts to show that Jesus leaves it at the age of thirty so that we may enter into it! He experiences a baptism that will take the form of his death on the cross and of his resurrection; he applies the fruits to us at Pentecost so that all humans may become children of the Holy Family. The Father wants to make us enter freely there where he formed his Son, since by the blood of his beloved Son we become his sons. Our baptism allows us to enter through the door Jesus used to come out: it is the crossroad of the destinies of the one who is God and becomes man among sinners, on the one hand, and on the other, of the sinners that we are. Jesus' baptism is, so to speak, a starting point, the beginning of "the times when Jesus walked as our head" (cf Ac 2:22).

We must find Nazareth in our own personal style, with our possibilities, and our original vocation. My Nazareth is unlike that of Charles de Foucauld although it is much indebted to it: how could one not love such a radical venture? How could one not feel that he is the spiritual son of Father Huvelin, especially when he writes that Jesus himself is the one who builds this spiritual Nazareth in us with his two hands? His two hands which, to us, gradually become less abstract, for they are especially real (spiritually), personalized, living!

To learn to live in Nazareth means to discover again the secrets that the prophets of Israel like Isaiah, for instance, suggested: "For thus says the Lord God, the Holy One of Israel: In returning and rest you shall be saved; in quietness and in trust shall be your strength. But you refused" (Is 30:15).

Conversion, tearing away from the falsified world of evil and deceit is Joseph's specialty, Joseph who makes us "die" to the folly of sin. The calm state of the obedient and inhabited heart is that of Mary subjected to her husband. The perfect trust in the love of the Father is what Jesus lives for us.

In the same frame of mind, we can read Micah's admirable text (6:8), the answer to those ready for anything, even for criminal follies in order to make God favorable to them: "He has told you, O mortal, what is good; and what does the Lord require of you but to do justice, and to love kindness, and to walk humbly with your God?" Joseph, the "righteous" man, is the guide for the first point, Mary for the second and Jesus realizes the third to perfection.

In Joseph, one naturally lives, as it were, these wonders as indispensable as they are impossible for the complicated and wounded humans that we are, and lives them in a practical way, at the level "of the feet and the hands." From the first moments of the "apparitions," Bernadette has to learn a new way of making the sign of the Cross, of greeting, of making acts of penance.

Indeed, man is invited to a new way of thinking by this unique master: he does not speak as if he did not think but he does exactly all he should. Thought is no longer a master here, as it almost always is; it is a humble servant of a design beyond itself. A stumbling-block for the proud! A wonder for the humble heart! Reason finds its true place and so do the angels. An important place! In Joseph, they have nothing to fear, they will not be imitated: they can make us intelligent without our becoming proud, since we know we have received these lights; they can initiate us to loving kindness without our losing our sense of respect; to intimacy without our ignoring distances; to liberty without our renouncing to a perfect control of ourselves; to trials without our being crushed (cf 2 Cor 4:7-8).

Only those admitted by Joseph will enter into the intimacy of the Holy Family: shepherds, Magi, Simeon, Anna. Those whom he mistrusts like the indiscreet, Herod's soldiers who wish to harm his Child, are kept at a distance. They either ignore what is going on or else they are helpless.

To become a son of Joseph, to imitate what the father does (cf Jn 5:19) is a very simple way of directing one's mental life by slipping out of one's thoughts, out of interior locutions, out of various impressions so that these potential "spiritual enemies" (cf Ep 6:12) have no longer any ways of access. Short moments of quiet, of control, of presence to real impressions are much more precious than one might think; they help us tear ourselves away from panic, from negative thoughts, from dangerous distractions. It is an art of which everyone must be aware for it is essential, an art everyone must exercise through simple efforts, the first being to breathe as calmly as possible. The other elementary efforts to be learned are related to the way in which sensations are experienced: to see what is before our eyes, to touch really what is at hand, to listen to a light sound, if possible as natural as the wind, water or the song of a bird. All these humble exercises draw the human soul away from dangerous influences, on which it has little hold, and open it to divine influence. One can say that Mary is the Queen of angels through whom the divine influence is usually transmitted at the mental level. Joseph is the filter of the angels: to enter again into his silence and his night, for some time, is to allow an astonishing decantation.

If indeed, as St. Paul says at the end of the Letter to the Ephesians, our true enemies "are not of flesh and blood," that is, are not other humans but these perverted spirits which perturb us and lead us astray, one can suppose that Mary would want humans of today to discover how to make this filter work.

With Joseph, when we are truly united with Christ, the Devil fears us, says St. John of the Cross. Otherwise, he deceives us.

Jacques Maritain has said: "There will always be a growing number of truths and a growing number of lies." Words of a true thinker, words that have more depth than a well! Certainly, many truths are displayed in every field of knowledge, techniques are developed but sometimes with the speed of avalanches, in a deadly way, because human wisdom does not keep abreast of the level of the intelligence, as Henri Bergson already deplored in his great work, *The Two Sources of Morality and Religion*. The ambiguities, the approximations, the errors, the illusions, and the deadly ideologies proliferate at the same time as undeniable discoveries.

That is why, with every day that goes by, a proper awareness of the protection that the Father wants to give us in Joseph as he did for Jesus becomes more and more desirable.

2. AN EASY YOKE, A LIGHT BURDEN

Upon reflection, one discovers that the art being sought consists in living a mysterious maxim from St. John of the Cross: "One single thought of man is of greater worth than the whole world; wherefore God alone is worthy of it."[1] One senses that nothing should hamper true human liberty, the one that comes from the Spirit of God, but what the fact of "thinking of God" concretely consists in is not so obvious.

It is there that the Holy Family offers a baffling answer: God is simplicity; God is realism; God is in the manger, in the flight to Egypt, in the workshop. God is in the daily struggle to survive, even if we do not always rise to lofty heights, when we are dogged by illness, creditors, a difficult spouse, provided we live in a certain state of mind. Provided there is a tiny little space for hope, that is, a certain form of courage and detachment so often present, in fact, in poor human endeavors.

There is a very simple way of struggling, in our down-to earth existence, in our daily routine: it goes back to the core of the Gospel and the fatherhood of Joseph, without our becoming aware of this. Jesus led this relentless war against evil in all its forms and he learned how to do this in Nazareth throughout the long years he spent there.

If Mary succeeds in introducing us to this art, we will think less and act more, without falling into activism in the slightest way. We shall learn to perform the necessary actions silently, in a silence which is not only exterior but also interior, as Bernadette did. "He says nothing and thinks less!" says the humorist. But things are happening. And in the heart of this silence, there is a conviction: Christ is there through his Holy Spirit without my being aware of him in the least. I simply believe he is. He is the one who, in fact, acts through me, speaks, loves, forgives. A conviction which hardly takes the form of a thought; it is so profound, so obscure, undefined although indisputable. There, without a doubt, we find the intuition of St. John of the Cross, like that of Napoleon who, in the domain he knew, proclaimed one truth: "War is a simple art which exists only in execution."

"My yoke is easy, and my burden is light" (Mt 11:30). Indeed, it is only a matter of performing a series of elementary actions, each being relatively simple, sometimes very simple, childish. It is there that divine majesty and its entire court are waiting for us. Here, there are no longer little things since the great ones, without the first, would not exist (cf Lk 19:17). But, sometimes, one must make great decisions, excruciating ones. In any case, the one who wishes to live in the shadow of Joseph feels he is gliding into a world of joy, liberty, hidden beauty, friendship where everything conspires to dispose the soul favorably, to comfort it, encourage it to continue, to give it some flexibility and patience (what I call "divine magic").

A light burden, says Jesus again. It is a burden for, here, selfishness is impossible and difficulties soon weigh us down, not only our own but those of others as well. Nothing is centered on the individual any more, everything becomes personal, in relation to other persons. But here also, a certain new power of discernment (so as not to be absorbed, abused, dispossessed), a certain force of realism, a dynamism, a cheerfulness that comes from we know not where, make much lighter what could have appeared overwhelming, even impossible. The most unprecented and important impulse comes from friendship. Nothing lightens more the heaviest of loads; the saints constantly say so with St. Augustine: where there is love, "either there is no pain or the pain itself is loved." And in human beings, God is again the one who is loved, "for it is my opinion that I love nothing else but God, and all the souls for God."[2] And the love that humble creatures have for us comes from the Almighty.

The Holy Spirit, the Spirit of Jesus, since Jesus gives humans this Spirit as he himself received it from the Father (cf Jn 20:21), loves to create for us the conditions the Father wanted for the Son. They culminate in Joseph's indisputable simplicity, the first rung of the ladder to paradise, as St. Leonard of Porto Maurizio would say.

No one should say he is unworthy, that he is unable, that he does not know, since God is the one who does everything when we let him as did Joseph who, precisely, could do only just that. The art of becoming like children!

In the case of St. Bernadette, for instance, a falsified humility will often make us say: "Ah! But she was a saint!" Each one of us must become an original saint, indispensable. God wanted this "daughter of Joseph" to be led "by ordinary ways," as the superiors of Nevers would say not without some disappointment, so that no one might reject her, as too grandiose or extraordinary destinies would incite them to do. Let us aim at the simplest and most ordinary and God will be able to do whatever he wishes, something which is never lacking in interest. Let us aim at Martha, the one who is hostess to Jesus, and we can anticipate meeting Mary, the contemplative one at the feet of the Lord. In fact, St. Teresa of Avila speaks in this way in the seventh Mansion of her Castle, at the summit, at the center: Martha and Mary are there each as important and worthy as the other.

Meanwhile, let us look to this father given to us by God and shown to us by Mary. We shall see three aspects in him:

— he does not speak but teaches us a certain silence;
— he is not seen and Jesus totally disappears in his hands; he holds the secret of the night;
— one must remain with him: he teaches us to make the most of time.

3. SILENCE

Enlightened minds know that silence will be the language of heaven. Already on earth it is the condition for essential communication: "One word spoke the Father, which word was his Son, and this word he speaks ever in eternal silence, and in silence must it be heard by the soul."[3]

That is why the Psalm points out that the language of heaven, both day and night, is a silent language, "there is no speech . . . heard" (Ps 19:3).

To find again something of this hidden language, to communicate beyond words, is to find again the secret of the Holy Family; it is to escape from a multitude of misunderstandings, of complications, even of illnesses. It is to open oneself to unknown possibilities of intellectual, poetic, love expression. That is why St. John of the Cross points out: "That which we most need in order to make progress is to be silent before this great God, with the desire and with the tongue, for the language that he best hears is that of silent love."[4]

The Spanish mystic ties in with a medical doctor of the beginning of this century, Roger Vittoz (died in 1925), a Protestant of great depth, the author of a method of psychic control which is a masterpiece of simplicity and efficacy, the *Vittoz Method*. It teaches mainly what Joseph is in charge of making known to all humans: the art of eliminating — eliminating idle thoughts, not by fighting them off but by gently slipping out of their hold, of their implacable logic, as Joseph slipped away from the clutch of Herod's soldiers. To fight against evil thoughts, when teaching in the temple, is the best way of making them still more obsessive, more dangerous. Let us leave the task of facing up to the forces of evil to St. Michael; with Joseph who is but a human being as we are, let us learn the precious art of evasion. It is the art practiced by Jesus at the time of his first confrontation with Satan.

How can one escape the evidence of pride which underscores the superiority of this one, the insignificance of that one, going easily from one to the other to arrive in both cases to the same inflexibility? How can one escape from the morbid suggestions of the senses, from attraction for alcohol, drugs or very simply, from the fatal return of fixed ideas? How can one escape this obsessive past where the Devil easily finds ways of accusing his unfortunate victims, by night and by day, before the throne of God (cf Rv 12:10)? (Too often, this victim in question agrees with these accusations and thinks that no one else but God could stir up so many truths).

If we learn to practice interior silence with the one who does not speak and who is in charge of teaching it to us, we will be amazed to see mountains slide away and disappear (cf Mk 9:29).

The principle of the operation consists in replacing, at a point in time, our mental logic, whatever power and coherence it may have, by a true sensation: what I touch, what I really hear outside of myself (not inside); the ground under my feet, the tree standing before my eyes that I must learn to see "with the candor of a young calf" (What an art, especially for an intellectual!). Everything is good to pull us away from this drama we call "thought," not without a remarkable lack of awareness. Scripture often warns us that the thoughts of humans are obscure and vain.

What does not come from God, as all masters of spirituality have noted, from St. Catherine of Siena to St. John of the Cross, is often brilliant, inspiring at first, then becomes a source of uneasiness, sadness, perturbation. What comes from God is often quite bitter, exercises little attraction at first but quickly becomes a source of profound peace. It is this unique acknowledged fact that struck the young Ignatius of Loyola so much when he was comparing the impression made on him, in turn, by the things of this world and those he found in the lives of saints. This truth, when acknowledged, is the essence of the art of discerning, according to his *Spiritual Exercises*. Now then, it suffices for us to give a little silence to our soul so that these principles of discernment may function on their own and with what clarity!

We must find the ways of silence in ourselves beginning as we have said in passing, with breathing:[5] to breathe calmly while becoming aware of the symbolic aspects of the operation is, so to speak, the first spiritual initiative, the first form of intelligent obedience of the creature to its Creator. To breathe out with Joseph, (the patron saint of the art of expiring, of eliminating, of dying) in order to breathe in the same way with Mary (the woman inhabited by the Spirit, source of all "inspiration," divine breath). Breathing thus experienced becomes like the balancing pole of the tightrope walker, which allows him to move forward on his rope without falling. Breathing is the only psychic reality on which we have a direct hold to help us cross certain difficult passages where we run the risk of panicking, getting lost, and allowing ourselves to be alienated (with the complicity of the powers of darkness to which one must not give the slightest importance, but whose harmful effects it would be ridiculous to ignore).

4. THE NIGHT OF FAITH

There are two limits to human attention: that of the man who falls asleep, yielding himself to the biological wisdom hidden in the innermost recesses of his being and which alone can restore him in depth; that of the man who touches the edges of "ecstasy" because he has caught a glimpse of beauty, of love, of true prayer. When man forgets himself to become attention, this other mysterious being, "the Holy Spirit, intercedes with sighs too deep for words, praying for what man does not know how to ask" (cf Rm 8:26) as the Apostle says.

We have here, as it were, two kinds of surrender, two forms of death to oneself.

These are like two poles between which human life unfolds itself in its most ordinary, trivial daily aspect. But if we wish this daily life to flourish within the framework of the Holy Family, it must also have its "mortifications," as it was said in the past. "If you live according to the flesh, you will die; but if by the Spirit you put to death the deeds of the body, you will live" (Rm 8:13).

Thus there are three kinds of death, perfectly coordinated, by which the patron saint of a happy death opens up the treasures of the new Wisdom, Jesus himself, that Mary keeps for us. Blessed is the one who knows in what direction to look for these treasures! "For you have died," says St. Paul, "and your life is hidden with Christ in God" (Col 3:3); blessed is the one who has had a glimpse — he knows not how — of the place where God keeps Christ hidden on earth in the night of faith.

In order to give a perfectly concrete turn to the process of learning to which we must subject ourselves, nothing is more instructive than to meditate on the first and the most elementary of these three forms of death, the art of lending ourselves to sleep.

Bergson used to say in one of his famous expressions, "to sleep is to let things go." Man lets go his usual mental experience for the sake of an interest of prime importance: that of recuperating in depth, of allowing God to restore him.

The moment a man stretches out on his bed, after having gently prepared himself by casting aside in time all that could make him restless, is essential because sleep is essential. Those who sleep with ease generally do not suspect that this moment is important or, at least, their awareness of this is not as convincing as it is for those who have experienced difficult periods of insomnia. Whatever that may be, the essential nature of sleep is linked not only to its importance at the level of human stability but also to its value as a symbol, to the exemplary teachings to which it corresponds.

Like Jesus sleeping in the middle of the storm, sleep expresses a perfect trust in God who "neither slumbers nor sleeps" (cf Ps 121:4) and who takes care of us all the more since we let him do so. That is why the Lord makes the harvest of the just man grow, instructs Joseph about his secret wishes during his sleep, suggests a totally dedramatized image of death for the death of the just ("the girl is not dead but sleeping" [cf Mt 9:24]; the same for Lazarus). But one must go further. The effort which the one seeking sleep must make when he does not easily drop off to sleep,[6] in contrast with the happy mortal of the Psalm who "lies down and sleeps" (cf Ps 3:5) right away, is a typical example. It is, as it were, the model of all spiritual effort.

We should have two different positions when in bed:

— the position of reflection, reading, conversation, prayer — where our head does not touch the sheet (one can, for example, be either in the sitting position or be stretched out with his hands at the back of his head);
— the sleeping position: the head is resting on the pillow. In this second position, no form of thought or even of prayer in the sense generally given to the word (that is, a form of conscious mental activity) is tolerable for it is directly opposed to trying to fall asleep. One either thinks or sleeps.

Actually, the whole body becomes an imploration by lending itself to this incomparable gift of natural sleep, a gift which comes down from the Father to restore us, to instruct us, to renew us, to comfort us as needed and to draw us away from daily anxieties which threaten our psychic life.

In order to promote a happy descent into sleep, one must gently and patiently come away from any continuous line of thought by concentrating on basic sensations, a foot, a leg, a hand, the wrapping of a sheet, a vague rumor or, very simply, by allowing oneself to sway to the rhythm of one's own breathing like the few-month-old child. Letting oneself go, not choosing one's position in bed. There is in us a wisdom that knows so much more than we do when we give it free rein!

During sleep, as scientists have studied closely these last years, nature alternates phases of dreamless sleep with short periods of dreaming which are particularly beneficial. All of that takes place within ourselves and is, in some way, beyond our direct control.

The same conclusions apply to this form of deep prayer taught in a masterly way by St. Teresa of Avila in her writings: the meditative prayer of which, as she explains in chapter 6 of her autobiography, St. Joseph is the expert. There is nothing surprising in that, since to pray in meditation is to leave behind our habitual mode of thinking in order to enter mysteriously into communication with the Beloved. It is not a matter of finding oneself again but of losing oneself, exactly as when one is trying to drop off to sleep. The effort made to relax, the forgetfulness of self, the subtle checking out of one's thoughts and habitual logic is exactly the same process.

And there also, in the same way that sleep comes upon us without our being able to do anything directly to bring it about, this communication can be established with the Lord, and be for us a source of benefits absolutely out of proportion with the efforts we have made.

All is gift. Nothing is automatic, no technique is infallible, neither to sleep, to pray, or to make oneself loved. This is exactly what magic seeks, what the gurus and the sects deceitfully promise. No, God is Spirit and the Spirit is liberty, conditioned by absolutely nothing. But if we know how to act like trusting little children, then this fatherly liberty can refuse us nothing: "If you then, who are evil, know how to give good gifts to your children, how much more will the heavenly Father give the Holy Spirit to those who ask him!" (Lk 11:13).

5. THE MENTAL AND THE SPIRITUAL

Indeed, it is a matter of opening oneself to the Holy Spirit, to the Spirit of the Son who came from the Father, and that is all there is to that. Everything, without exception, in the human adventure is reduced to this Gift of gifts which contains all things as St. Seraphim of Sarov used to think. We never directly feel the presence of the Holy Spirit for there is nothing in our awareness that is naturally proportioned to deal with God. St. John of the Cross and all the masters of spirituality insist on this point and rightly so.

Better yet, as Monsieur Olier's last spiritual director, Father de Condren would say, the more God approaches a human being, the less the human being feels him for the approach is increasingly

spiritual, therefore, decreasingly accessible to the senses. God
loves to give strong impressions to beginners to draw them to him,
encourage them, like the unforgettable memories sometimes experienced in a retreat, a pilgrimage, an encounter. But, little by
little, one must learn to live in a kind of austerity where faith alone
reaches what it firmly holds without seeing or feeling anything.

"Love consists not in feeling great things," says St. John of the
Cross, "but in having great detachment and in suffering for the
Beloved."[7]

In some way, one must develop the habit of going from a
mental activity, corresponding to our clear awareness, to what we
feel, what we mentally recall, imagine, sense in our body or in our
psyche, to a spiritual life where everything is apparently abolished.

This transfer is not easy: it is but a variation on the theme which
is central to our study, the descent from Jerusalem to Nazareth;
Jerusalem, the image of mental life as "religious" as one could
wish, as rich as one could hope, and Nazareth, the image of a
spiritual life, detached, silent, obscure. No, this transfer is not easy
but, fortunately, as the angel said, "Nothing is impossible with
God" (cf Lk 1:37).

When one senses his presence, thanks to Mary, Joseph appears
to me to be the master of this delicate transfer.

People will perhaps be surprised to know that I do not often
address prayers to Joseph, while I am deeply aware that I pray only
in him. I do think of him (what could my thinking be focused on?)
but he teaches me, precisely, the art of not thinking "in the human
way," a way which so often saddened Jesus when he was with his
apostles (cf Mt 16:23).

Let us consider an example: the more someone is dear to us, the
less we have to think of that person. We must reach him on a
spiritual level whether he is present or absent, and not through our
imagination, daydreams or a set of impressions we interpose. The
mental faculty must be at the service of the operation with the
greatest discretion possible: it must not act as a screen, capturing,

arresting, and all the more so, distorting. We must realize that unless a kind of miracle takes place, things are bound to be so.

The human mental faculty is intrusive and, moreover, it is falsified most of the time, except in a tiny child and in those who end up by being like children after a long period of purification. Never were Jesus' words so true: "No one is good but God alone!" (Lk 18:19). Human imagination, memory, feelings and the rest are a field of darnel dramatically mixed up with the good grain and it is preferable that we leave it so, as Jesus says. The more the affective aspect of our nature is unleased in what we call love or its opposites (anger, indignation, jealousy, fear, etc.), the more the mental aspect becomes delirious, tyrannical, dangerous, the more it risks falsifying objective reality.

What shall we say about fixed ideas, obsessions and other analogous difficulties which are so dramatically widespread?

Joseph teaches us the supreme art of dying to our mental life in order to allow ourselves to be born again to a way of perfection which is akin to that of Mary and is only remotely similar to what we could have known previously. Let us, for some time, try the experiment of never deliberately recalling the human being we love very much; we will then begin to realize that love comes from much beyond, from a much greater depth than our human heart alone, our feelings, our judgment, whatever qualities they may have. We will experience a freedom so new, an insight, a loving force so ingenious that we will no longer be able to deny that all comes from elsewhere.

St. John of the Cross, this accomplished son of the Carmel of the house of Mary and Joseph, had said as much but it was difficult to believe him.

"Take no heed of the creatures if thou wilt keep the image of God clearly and simply in thy soul, but empty thy spirit of them, and withdraw far from them, and thou shalt walk in the Divine light, for God is not like to the creatures."[8]

Inhuman? Impossible? Only those who have tried for some

158 St. Joseph: Shadow of the Father

time can truly speak about this. Indeed, they understand that it is by such roads that one reaches what was being so poorly sought, in the manner of impatient and domineering humans or of those who daydream too much. St. Francis de Sales understood that God makes us reach our goals when we pursue them like oarsmen, by turning our backs to them.

6. LEANING ON TIME

The newness of time, the true one, the one that comes from God alone, he who "makes all things new" (cf Rv 21:5) was the secret of Joseph and of his impossible mission. He was progressively, successively, warned of what he had to do, as is seen in Matthew's or Luke's Gospel. Time, the Father's secret, disposed him interiorly to face his disconcerting trials of every moment. Time accompanied him lovingly in order to allow him to face the unique period in the history of humanity when God slowly became man.

Joseph had to put to work the "perseverance" recommended by Jesus as the secret of life (cf Lk 8:15; 21:19), the attitude of heart described by St. Paul as the "steadfastness of hope in our Lord Jesus Christ" (1 Th 1:3). He can now show us how to place our trust in time (since God works in time), without ever controlling it: "It is not for you to know the times or periods that the Father has set by his own authority" (Ac 1:7), he could say as did Jesus. To live intelligently with time is a superior art that Joseph eminently learned in the company of Mary, then of Jesus, in particular. But they also, mysteriously, wanted to learn it with him.

What is certain is that the time lived within the Holy Family is always a constructive, positive time, directed toward life, for the silence and night of God, entrusted to Joseph, link him up with eternity. Even if appearances seem otherwise, we are certain of one thing: time works in our favor. One has but to believe this for some time to see the promises appear, promises which are not always like the ones we had anticipated, far from it! Joan of Arc had understood she would be freed by "a great victory," but she could not forsee that this meant she would be burnt at the stake in Rouen.

One should learn, without any sense of fatalism, to lean on time as the bird leans on the air and the child Jesus on the arms of Joseph.

Besides, biblical authors used the image of the eagle or of the vulture to evoke fatherly protection:

> In a howling wilderness waste . . .
> As an eagle stirs up its nest,
> and hovers over its young;
> as it spreads its wings, takes them up,
> and bears them aloft on its pinions (Dt 32:10-11).

Why not see in this eagle the one who protects the woman in chapter 12 of Revelation, that is, the one who protects the Church, each one of us, the very image of the Father protecting his family as Joseph effectively protected the early Church? God is faithful, God is consistent: what he has done, he does again. It is through the one recognized by the Church as the patron saint of the universal Church that the Father wants to protect the Church of his Son of which Mary is the figure, the Mother.

> The woman was given the two wings of the great eagle,
> so that she could fly from the serpent into the wilderness,
> to her place where she is nourished
> for a time, and times, and half a time (Rv 12:14).

What does this apparently obscure passage mean? It seems to me that all we have examined offers a meaning which is acceptable and gradually becomes clearer.

This eagle is the image of time when it is lived as it should be, that is, as Jesus lived it, in complete trust in the Father. One can then truly say that time is grace. This goes back to the experience of

St. Teresa of Avila who knew that "patience obtains everything." In several passages, the Bible notes this relation between time and the eagle: Job laments over the fact that his days "flee away, they see no good, . . . like an eagle swooping on the prey" (Jb 9:25-26); the psalmist, on the contrary, is amazed by the freshness of God's gifts, always new, "so that your youth is renewed like the eagle's" (Ps 103:5). The eagle well portrays this divine patience full of tender care, that saves those who place their trust in it: "I bore you on eagles' wings," says the Lord, "and brought you to myself" (Ex 19:4).

The two wings of the great eagle are the secret of the true way of living time. These wings are the silence of the soul and the night of faith, that is, the two specialties of Joseph, the providential man chosen by the Father. The dragon is totally helpless against those who know how to obey Joseph, as Jesus did for so long, by observing these two essential points. Why? Because the dragon, the image of the Devil, is but a creature and, like every creature, he needs created elements to enable him to intervene in us and perturb us: he needs phantasms, drawn from our memory or our imagination, or again interior locutions like those which so often hum in poor human brains. That is enough for him to work out the greatest havoc. To learn the art so simple but so demanding of putting our poor head to silence, to place our trust during the night in the One who cannot fail us is to make the two wings of the great eagle function and save time by allowing the power of the cross to manifest itself. The cross is at the center of time: "Christ is the power of God, not only as the one sent by God, Son of God and God himself, but as the crucified one. For death on the cross is the means of salvation invented by the unfathomed wisom of God" (Edith Stein).

The radiance of the glorious cross is at the heart of our whole journey. Thanks to it, a new way of living time in the Holy Family brings out three advantages:

— the first is the density which the present moment assumes. It represents reality, therefore, the world of God, the only point of reference. It is better therefore to exercise the greatest vigilance on one's memory and imagination: "So do not worry about tomorrow, for tomorrow will bring worries of its own. Today's trouble is enough for today" (Mt 6:34);

— the second one is the divine solicitude set about to work for those who acknowledge themselves as little children. "All things work together for good for those who love God" (Rm 8:28). "All things" here must be understood literally: all things help us, all things build us. "Divine magic" is at our service to make servants of us and the more we believe this, the truer it is;

— the third one is the benefit of the "coincidence of contradictories." Time and eternity come together like the beginning and the end, the angel and man: angels can as early as today do their work of the last judgment, bind the darnel and the good grain in bales in our field. We begin to feel we are enlightened, uncluttered, simplified — without our knowing very well how.

All is paradoxical in this domain. For the one who learns to glide with Jesus on the Father's time as the bird glides on the air, the greatest catastrophes, the most horrible crashes assume another meaning: "Stand up and raise your heads, because your redemption is drawing near" (Lk 21:28).

O Joseph, teach us this incomparable art whereby the Spirit of the obedient Son of the Father triumphs, the art of leaning on the constant newness of the Father's time, whatever form it may take, assured as we are that it always supports us, guides us, and makes us grow even if at times we have the impression we are "walking on water," like Peter.

ANNEX: *THE TWO HANDS OF THE SON*

The prejudices against the all important place which is proper
to St. Joseph in the Christian mystery disappear as soon as we
consider a simple truth: like Mary, Joseph is an integral part of the
mystery of Christ in the same way that the hands are a part of the
body.

Certainly, one can enter into a relationship with someone else
without taking his hands into account. Each one of us is greater than
his hands. If the worst came to the worst, we could lose them, but
the tragedy entailed underscores their fundamental necessity. As a
rule, we do not do anything without our hands. Christ likes to act
through Joseph and Mary.

Already at the dawn of Christianity, St. Irenaeus had applied
this idea to the Father. "The Father," he said, "acts with his two
hands, his Son and his Spirit."

What is interesting to note in passing is the extreme difference
between each of these two hands and the perfect harmony of their
double intervention.

The Son is the Word by which the Father calls beings into
existence, "each according to its kind," as is expressed in
Genesis. Starting from the primeval chaos, this Word will determine distinctive traits in each of the innumerable creatures by
assigning a particular shape and role to each. That is why Scripture
compares it to a "two-edged sword, piercing until it divides soul
from spirit, joints from marrow, it is able to judge the thoughts and
inventions of the heart" (Heb 4:12). That is why the Jewish Law
forbids mixtures which would lead to confusion, to chaos: cross-
breeding, hybrids, harnessing different animals together,
homosexuality which ignores sexual differences. These practices
make man regress to the primeval chaos. As soon as the Son has
brought these different creatures into being, as soon as the Word
has brought them into existence by giving distinctive traits to
each, the Spirit excels in making its own combinations which are

so harmonious in contrast with formless mixtures: its crowning masterpiece is the loving unity of man and woman, "the image and likeness" of God himself. It is the Spirit that weds the spiritual with the carnal, instinct with reason, hydrogen with oxygen.

Similarly, how could one not see that the Spirit himself has two hands by which he constantly joins the human beings that we are: the angels and the saints. There again, the processes of action are radically opposed: the angel is endowed with an infallible intuition as quick as lightning; its knowledge is perfectly coherent; the saint is a being of clay, shuffling about, who slowly, obscurely constructs the fragile little world of his knowledge. With Joseph and Mary, in the New Jerusalem, as we have said, angels communicate their lights to the saints and the saints provide a channel of expression for the angels, an expression of which they are otherwise deprived. A marvellous collaboration without which the saints would know nothing of interest and the angels could not express themselves.

Certainly, the Holy Spirit unites himself in person to the one who opens himself to charity (cf Rm 5:5): "Anyone united to the Lord becomes one spirit with him" (1 Cor 6:17). Without this Spirit, we cannot "belong to Christ" (cf Rm 8:9). But in order that this Spirit may come and remain, two conditions are necessary: Joseph and Mary, the two hands of Christ.

The action of these two hands is condensed in one verse from St. Paul: "If we have died with Christ, we believe that we will also live with him" (Rm 6:8). We recognize there the baptismal mystery: this sacrament of prime importance, thanks to an expressive gesture, make man experience death to sin and resurrection to a new life.

Joseph, "our father and the patron saint of a holy death," as Bernadette used to say, teaches us death and Mary teaches us new life, her secret, and that all things come from Christ.

The world to which we must die is the world of distraction, not in the sense of entertainment but in the sense of a diversion. Sin diverts us, ourselves and all our energies, all our potential, from the true purpose of our existence which is love.[9] The world to which we must open ourselves is that of attention in which Mary excels. Joseph is the anti-distraction so that Mary may become in us a constantly renewed attention.

Let us sum up the whole process:

"The Father gives all things into the hands of the Son" (cf Jn 13:3).

The Holy Spirit is the one who assures this transfer in all its dimensions, in all its aspects, which are of interest to the slightest workings of creation, to the least of men's thoughts. That is what the angels and saints work at tirelessly under his direction.

Jesus builds his Church with his two hands.

Mary, Queen of angels and Mother of all saints, prepares the hearts of men so that her Son may come down in them.

But the last one, the one who gives the final touch, the essential preparation by turning aside the subtle dangers in the realm of the spiritual of which we are far from making an adequate assessment, is most often the hand of Joseph.

He is at the end of this incomparable chain which starts from the Father and which returns to him. He is the humble first link: it is from him that we must first, in the innermost recesses of our heart, learn to obey.

---

1   *The Complete Works of St. John of the Cross*, op. cit., vol. 3, *Spiritual sentences and maxims*, no. 32, p. 222.

2   We recognize here one of Saint Francis de Sales' ideas, quoted earlier.

3   *The Complete Works of St. John of the Cross*, op. cit., vol. 3, *Points of Love*, no. 21, p. 228.

4   *Ibid.*, no. 53, p. 232.

5   Father Déchanet has devoted a book on these subjects, which has become a classic. Its title is *The Ways of Silence*.

6   Unfortunately, it is a well known fact that in our restless times, so far removed from the habits inspired by ancient common sense, we experience much difficulty in sleeping. Millions of people now resort to pharmaceutical products.

7 *The Complete Works of St. John of the Cross*, op. cit., vol. 3, *Points of Love*, no. 36, p. 230.
8 *Ibid., Spiritual sentences and maxims*, no. 25, p. 221.
9 "The one thing that comforts us in our miseries is diversion and, nevertheless, it is the greatest of our miseries" (Pascal, *Pensées*, Brunschvicg ed., 171).

CHAPTER VIII

Conclusion

1. A ROUTE

AS we come to the end of this route, to the discovery of Joseph, Monsieur Olier's thought comes back to my mind and I find that I agree more profoundly with it than I did at the beginning: "In my opinion, this saint is beyond what can be understood by the minds of men." The more progress I make, the more the mystery thickens in a way but the dearer it becomes to me; the greater it appears to me, it is more actual, more indispensable. Not for one minute have I stopped depending on it and I have made progress. I have also helped brothers and sisters to get a glimpse of it, to enter with courage into this cloud, so simple and so demanding, and they have found a little more peace and light; they have experienced a new possibility of enjoying liberty. When one is bound hand and foot, burdened; when everything seems dark, leading to a dead end, without any solution in sight and time is fatally running against one, what an odd impression it is to realize that a new break is possible, that a remission exists, that a little joy and freedom can still bring a totally different meaning to life!

The need to have someone speak about this is no longer as great in the person, who, for a certain amount of time, has experienced this form of simplification and protection hidden in St. Joseph's fatherhood, when this ingenious, respectful, effective power is put to work. An internal device, a kind of inner structure, very demanding and very gentle, falls into place and starts to operate in him. He begins to fear distraction in his mind, mental vagrancy; he no longer listens to the suggestions of his sensitivity in the way he used to. He gives the greatest importance to attention.

The words of Jesus, "My yoke is easy and my burden is light" take on a concrete meaning, as if he were telling us: "Take my parents as your parents, carry on the experiment I made with them, since all that is mine is yours now!"

It will be interesting to be able to exchange one's impressions when such a way of seeing and living will have become more widespread: in this incomparable world, no one can boast about anything. Each is urged to share what he is aware of having received. St. Paul quotes one of Jesus' sayings which is not explicitly mentioned in the Gospels: "It is more blessed to give than to receive" (Ac 20:35). Jesus is the first to acknowledge that he received from the Father all that he has the joy of giving us. Mary sings this joy in the Magnificat. What could be said of Joseph, the humble carpenter?

In the Holy Family, there is an art of sharing which is absolutely worthy of imitation. The Bible tells us that Joseph is instructed by the angel during the night. Thanks to these divine admonitions, he can fulfil his particular duties, step by step, and everyone obeys him. As for Jesus, he wants to rely entirely on Mary and Joseph, two human beings to whom his Father has entrusted him. What a mysterious interplay! It should function in our lives today, to our greatest joy and benefit.

The Holy Family has indeed taken its full dimension in heaven: Joseph welcomes Mary, his wife, with him in heaven in view of the mystery of the begetting of the Body of Christ. According to St. Francis de Sales' firm conviction, her assumption appears to be part of the simple logic of things.

To acknowledge Joseph's fatherhood and, consequently, to imitate this father, as Jesus did, is simply to discover the demands made on Christians at the level of "the feet and the hands," and not in words, in justifications which, in the words of Péguy, are often "compromises" ("we compromise when we resort to explanations rather than to actions"). St. Joseph teaches us the art of thinking less in order to be more intelligent; the art of feeling less in order to be more loving according to the very tradition of the Carmel born in his hands on August 24, 1562.

> In order to arrive at having pleasure in everything,
> Desire to have pleasure in nothing.
> In order to arrive at possessing everything,
> Desire to possess nothing . . .
> When thy mind dwells upon anything,
> Thou art ceasing to cast thyself upon the All.[1]

All these things are totally incomprehensible, like Joseph himself, when viewed from the outside. How everything changes as soon as one begins to enter there! To enter, one must sometimes be helped a little, urged on a little by some trial or some unforgettable encounter.

Certain human beings, like John XXIII, Bernadette or Brother André seem predestined to make these discoveries because of their background, their character; others, like Marcel Callo, by their condition as laborers. It is moving to note that, in the style of Bernadette, he leaves Rennes, his city, to protect his father from the harassments of the Gestapo on March 19, 1943. He sets out as a laborer for the S.T.O. (the compulsory labor service) but, especially, as a missionary. He will die emaciated, tortured in a concentration camp, but at peace, unfailingly meek, on March 19, 1945.

May all these witnesses of yesterday and today help the Church to discover the new face of the Father through Joseph as Jesus did.

2. *DISCERNMENT*

The weak point in a certain recent way of presenting Christianity lies in the absence of an essential component, nevertheless present everywhere in the Word of God as it is in reality: the invisible world, made up of invisible creatures about which the Gospel and St. Paul speak constantly, who are in charge of making God's message personal to us and of offering our prayer to God. There are also those spirits originally created by God and forever subjected to him in some way but who have become living lies, enemies of all true life, our real enemies (cf Ep 6:12). These two kinds of creatures are in fact in no way comparable: the angels who said yes to God are consistent spiritual realities who construct, who participate in an active way in the building of the Church. "The no said to God breaks down, destroys the inner unity and coherence without which a person cannot really be true to himself. We are mistaken therefore when we ask if Satan is a person; we are also mistaken if we reply that he certainly is not a personal being. He is a being who does not hold together because he is the act of saying no, an act which disintegrates everything including himself. He acts like a madman who would affirm himself by killing everybody if he could and end up by killing himself."[2]

These "spirits of the power of the air," as St. Paul calls them (cf Ep 2:2), have but the consistency we give them in our folly. If we allow them to have a hold on us, by means of evil thoughts, by not being vigilant about ourselves, they can become very harmful.

Today, in spite of an indisputable discovery of the Holy Spirit, the invisible world and its laws are much too ignored. We even ignore too much the extreme ambiguity of everything that touches the human mind and the spirits about which we never have any direct knowledge.

The spirits of the yes (those who obey the Queen of angels) are allies; they are so discreet, so simple, so coherent that we run the risk of ignoring them completely throughout our life like the healthy man who is oblivious of his liver.

The others seek to be forgotten, when they can, in order to promote, with impunity, these atmospheres of gloom, of doubt, of division, of suspicion or of mental obsessions which are so frequent. Sometimes, they put aside their masks when true dissociations of personalities occur, brought on by the use of alcohol, drugs, brutal violence; then they run the risk of unleashing a true infatuation with terror, with morbid interests. Let us leave aside the wayward ones who devote themselves to diabolical arts for purposes they would not dare admit.

Inasmuch as we little know how to open ourselves to the angels of God whose very existence we often ignore, so are we helpless in face of the other ones.

St. John of the Cross' doctrine on the matter is a masterpiece: it corresponds to what we have tried to expose by calling it "the descent of Nazareth." It is the art of escaping complications by secretly placing our trust in the Lord who can penetrate into our being, all doors being closed, as he did in the room where the apostles were hiding on the evening of Easter. The devil cannot do this.

"Test everything; hold fast to what is good" (1 Th 5:21). A precious advice but difficult to follow for it implies that the problem is solved, as we say: in order to put discernment into practice, one must be able to discern! That is why Joseph appears so helpful here: time discerns on its own as soon as we accept its silence and darkness.

3. LOVE

The Holy Family is meaningful only when related to Jesus "who gave himself for our sins to set us free from the present evil age, according to the will of our God and Father" (Gal 1:4). All things come from his love and all things lead to it: to be united with him and to be but one with him as he is one with the Father, this is what justifies the existence of the universe and the history of humankind. Mary, before whom the angel bows, stands aside before Jesus: "Do whatever he tells you" (Jn 2:5).

It is through her that the one St. Paul describes as the firstborn from the dead (Col 1:18) comes down to us. It is through Mary that God's promises reach us, "summed up" in Jesus Christ, and because of that she enjoys a privilege the Church has taken eighteen centuries to acknowledge, her Immaculate Conception. This total absence of sin, far from distancing her from the human race, on the contrary, makes her the creature closest to our hearts since sin alone alienates us from each other. But is it not through Joseph that these promises begin to be fulfilled? Does he not belong to this humanity, both miserable and sublime, which is ours, miserable in its profound reality and sublime inasmuch as it opens itself to the Spirit?

Here, we can move ahead only with yet greater precautions, for the Church has not defined anything. She does not know yet: having dared to pronounce her judgment on Mary, she has begun to do so on Joseph, as if the two spouses could not be separated from each other but the most important remains yet to be discovered.

Could we not think that Joseph was like us in every way? Surely, he was first a most attentive son of the Father since he was a "righteous" man, as the Scriptures say. Our experience in each one of us is clear: to be righteous among humans supposes many combats, sufferings, misunderstandings from those who are not so righteous.[3] Undoubtedly Joseph was not spared any of that.

Then he was the loving husband of an exceptional woman who, in turn, loved him most tenderly.

Finally, because of circumstances, he was the father of a child, outwardly like all the others, even if its reactions must have spoken to his soul, the soul of a father, a Jew and a believer, in depths which are beyond our powers of description. Silence alone is fitting.

A succession of realities as simple as they are unfathomable
make him both an ordinary and an absolutely extraordinary character as any Christian should be. It seems to me that he is, among all
men, the model as it were, inseparable from his wife, of those who
try to say yes to God with their whole being and whose every
response to divine friendship is found within his own.[4] On the one
hand, he is like us in every way; on the other, he is in a state that the
Church has been constantly discovering for centuries, not without
amazement: he maintains a unique and indefinable relationship
with the eternal Father.

That is why his status is so special. That is why "Go to Joseph;
what he says to you, do!" (Gn 41:55) resounds in history before
Mary's similar words, applied to Jesus, according to St. John. That
is why, in a harsh and corrupt world, which is totally "under the
power of the evil one" (1 Jn 5:19), the astuteness of the serpent,
subtle and silent, level with the ground (Joseph's specialty), is the
necessary introduction to the simplicity of the dove, where Mary
has no equal (cf Mt 10:16). That is why we must climb over the
walls of Jerusalem (Ps 122:7), that is, let go our pretensions, our
falsified logic, our pseudo-scientific systems or the deceptive revelations of sects, in order to have access to the palace of the true
loving Wisdom. That is why the door kept by Joseph, in this new
world of the Carmel, precedes the one kept by Mary. Finally, that
is why Mary places Joseph at the head, when Jesus makes his first
great choice on earth, a choice which will condition all the remain-
der of his life: "Your father and I have been searching for you in
great anxiety" (Lk 2:48). Words so mysterious, that Jesus himself
appears surprised!

O Joseph! Rare are the times when I speak to you so directly,
even though I take pains to obey you. I consider the fact of having
had a glimpse of your fatherhood to be a unique grace for I know it
contains everything: it represents this acceptance of the real in daily
life, this reality given by the eternal Father who, in his unfathomable love, loves to hide himself in you.

This fatherhood brings peace of heart and trust in faith, the irreplaceable atmosphere for other graces. It teaches us to reach Jesus hidden in the newness springing from the present moment.

It seems empty and silent, while it contains every memory and every Word. It seems cold and indifferent while it shelters Mary and all the sweetness of friendship. It makes us escape from all our enemies while it frees all the angels, necessary for our protection and spiritual instruction. Like the mysterious star before which others bow down, it draws all the Magi of the world and becomes the place for all research, since it is there that eternal Wisdom has fulfilled its most cherished wish, to dwell among the children of men (Pr 8:31).

Yes, through Mary and in her, Joseph, you become both the father of the Son and the "lieutenant" of the Father, and your secret dialogue unfolded itself in such an indescribable manner that nothing on earth can come near it, while all the steps we take in the Way, all Truth, all the true experiences of Life immerse us into it.

Bernadette adopts you as a father in an eternal "now." May we, in her footsteps, also discover the tiny gate and the narrow way that leads to life in order to become sons in the Son and savor, from now on, something of the eternal life turned toward the Father (cf 1 Jn 1:2).

ANNEX: *A REALIZATION*

If we wished to know what Joseph's world on this earth could be like today; if we wished to see with our own eyes an actual realization of Nazareth, we could contemplate, among others, the German work in Schoenstatt.

This institute, with its countless branches, spread in all the possible walks of life, was founded on October 18, 1914 by a twenty-nine-year-old German priest, Joseph Kentenich, a member

of the Congregation of the Pallottine Fathers.⁵ His Christian name
suited him well!

He wanted to live, in the very spirit of Jesus, a covenant of
love, of loving obedience with Mary, a moment to moment de-
pendence on the eternal Father (whom one feels very near, since he
manifests himself in all events). Precisely the mentality we have
attempted to describe of the one who, in Jesus, becomes ''son of
Joseph''! For him, it all began on the day he was named ''spiritual
father'' at the Pallotine College of Schoenstatt on October 27, 1912
(he was twenty-seven years old). Father Joseph Kentenich was an
exceptional spiritual father: a mind open to all areas of knowledge,
possessing courage, trust in Providence, audacity, a sense of innovation and initiative, thoughtfulness in love, an astonishing self-
control in the most agonizing of circumstances. The effectiveness,
the influence of his work earned him the distinction of being sent to
Dachau by the Nazis for three years and then to be persecuted by
men of the Church. Certain members of the postwar German
episcopate could not measure up to an action as powerful and
innovative as his which, they thought, cast umbrage on their own
pastoral work; they ended up by denouncing him to the Holy
Office.

Father Tromp, an eminent Jesuit, professor at the Gregorian,
the source of inspiration for the Encyclical *Mystici Corporis* and,
especially, an all-powerful consultant in the Holy Office, did not
understand the newness, the self-reliance and, in particular, this
note of divine intimacy in the style of the Holy Family which
characterized the movement. Entrenched in views that were too
rigid, too intellectual, too strongly influenced by the abstract
formulations of scholasticism, as Bérulle had been in the past with
respect to the Carmel, he failed to understand this life springing
forth, even if it was obviously blessed by God as the episopal
visitation had made clear.⁶ He sent this strong and calm man of
sixty-seven to exile in the United States, forbidding him to attend to

his institute which, in any case, he wanted to dissolve. The decree lay on the desk of the Pope who never signed it (1951).

Only at the age of eighty would he be authorized to return. In 1965, Paul VI received him with honor. His work had kept on growing during his absence. The proceedings for his beatification were begun in 1975, at the time when Father Tromp was being laid to rest.

Here is what he was telling his students in 1912:

... We are going to learn, under Mary's protection, to train ourselves to become men of a firm, free, priestly character.

... not only you but I as well. We shall learn from each other.

... not only in theory. That would not be of much use to us. No, we must learn also in practice, to get on with our work, every day, every hour.

How did we learn to walk? Did our mother give us long speeches? No, she took our hand, and on with it! One learns to walk by walking. That is the way we must learn to train ourselves, by constant practice.

This allusion to the mother was intentional. First, the Movement was a Marian movement of extraordinary scope for it extended over five continents through many diversified branches of activity (priests, religious, men and women, sick people, families, pilgrims, secular institutes, leagues). Far from altering the Movement, the ordeals its founder had undergone, had, on the contrary, made it stronger. A German bishop noted that all the priests of the Movement remained faithful to the Church and to their priestly commitment while the ranks of the clergy were being so terribly depleted during the '70's and so many priests left the priesthood.

What characterizes the Movement, in the first place, is a covenant of love with Mary of an unmatched audacity and conviction. This "Joseph" has complete faith in Mary: the term of the covenant of love each member must fulfil in a concrete, effective, profoundly personal way.

The Mother of God directs the work as a whole and each member in the details of his life, like the mother of a family, with the precision, the warmth and the totally divine respect for the liberties such as we witness in the courteous relationships between Mary and Bernadette in the Grotto of Lourdes. Liberty and autonomy are, so to speak, Schoenstatt's key ideas, with the specific Marian note which gives them their true color. Mary leads to Joseph. The Mother leads to the Father. Such is the second original aspect of the Movement, its truly new touch full of astonishing promises: it is totally turned to the Father. "Call no one your father on earth, for you have one Father — the one in heaven" (Mt 23:9), and St. Paul adds that it is from this Father that "every family in heaven and on earth takes its name" (Ep 3:15). Schoenstatt wants to put this wonder, fatherhood, to work.

The shirking of obligations in the role of fatherhood is one of the profound tragedies of our civilization. It is the absence of the father that makes so many individuals insecure, disoriented, profoundly unhappy and often dangerous.

Many priests have often ignored their spiritual fatherhood or refused to exercise it. It was confused with paternalism, authoritarianism or, worse yet, it raised fundamental suspicions.

To rediscover this indispensable fatherhood, strong, loving, enlightened, respectful of liberties, is to allow the eternal Father to communicate the most beautiful of his gifts, the least known and the most essential of his secrets. Jesus shows the reality of true fatherhood to us in a very special way in the parable of the Prodigal Son.

To make this fatherhood come from heaven down to the earth is the entire role of St. Joseph whom Joseph Kentenich in turn embodied.

This fatherhood alone can allow reason to play its role of

moderator of one's feelings and, consequently, bring forth all the riches, too little known, of the human soul and body. This fatherhood which represents the eternal Father allows reason, at least, to find in a faith beyond itself its true fulfillment without giving up any of its powers: "the measure of the progress in sciences must be the measure of our growth in inner depth, of our spiritual growth," as Joseph Kentenich was already saying in 1912.

An astonishing combination of strength and meekness! The Bishop of Treves laid emphasis on the "extraordinarily powerful religious spirit" which emanated from this founder. "Is it not possible that our little chapel might become our Tabor on which Mary's splendor might be manifested?" he said in 1914 at the very beginning of his work. This true spiritual father, in the very spirit of Joseph, his father, knew how to create this climate, so simple and so true, which made everything possible.[7]

FINAL WORD

One will perhaps understand at last St. John of the Cross' mysterious formula, the key to his whole work:

"In order to arrive at that which thou knowest not," that is, in order to enter into this unknown space, the very well guarded space of the eighteen years during which Jesus, the Child-God grew to the stature of the Son of Man, where the whole Gospel is elaborated; in order to penetrate into the place and time of all wonders.

"Thou must go by a way that thou knowest not,"[7] that is, become the sons and daughters of this silent man, so profoundly self-effaced, beyond our grasp, whom Mary alone really knows and shows us. You will see that he holds the secret to all lights, to all consistency, for it is to him that the Word, coming through Mary, was entrusted.

1 *The Complete Works of St. John of the Cross*, op. cit., vol. 1, *Ascent of Mount Carmel*, Book I, ch. 13, pp. 59-60.

2 E. Pousset, *Parole de Foi, Parole d'Église*, Droguet-Ardant, p. 85.

3 We are reminded of the sufferings of the young Joseph as related in the private revelations of Mary of Agreda, Catherine Emmerich or Maria Valtorta. We cannot assume these revelations to be facts but they do provide food for thought.

4 In one of the most astonishing books ever written about Saint Joseph, *St. Joseph intime*, which Pius X highly praised in his preface, the author Charles Sauvé writes: 'The Most Blessed Trinity takes more delight in him than in the angels and the saints.'

5 An excellent study of his life and work has been made by R. and A. Lejeune, *Schoenstatt chemin d'alliance*, St. Paul, 1985.

6 It is fatherhood that especially shocked Father Tromp.

7 *The Complete Works of St. John of the Cross*, op. cit., vol. 1, *Ascent of Mount Carmel*, Book I, ch. 13, p. 59.

Postscript

IN his famous thesis of 1893, *L'Action*, so little understood at the time, the philosopher Maurice Blondel describes, in an absolutely astonishing manner, the essence of the disconcerting communication between heaven and earth that Jesus was the first to experience. In him, we are called to live this communication through the same conditions as he did, in the life at Nazareth between Joseph and Mary where, effectively, a very simple action becomes the bearer of the whole divine mystery.

"It is from thought that it (faith) passes into the heart, it is from being put into practice that it draws a divine light for the mind. God operates in this action and that is why the thought that follows the act is richer by an infinity than the one preceding it. It is the entrance into a new world where no speculation can either lead it or follow it."